CW00507787

THE
GORNALS
Volume Two

NED WILLIAMS

For Jenny & Robert
Thanks for your
support

Ned Williams

Uralia Press

23 Westland Road, Wolverhampton, WV3 9NZ
2015

Front Cover: The "concert party" group that was based at St. James' Church, Lower Gornal between the wars. The identity of these players is explored later in the book. (Rhona Pickerill)
Back Cover: The Gornals have a new flag every year – designed by pupils in the local primary schools. In February 2015 Red Hall Primary School pupil Chloe Halford unveiled her flag outside the library in Gornal Wood in the presence of the Mayor Councillor Margaret Aston and organiser Dave Branwood. (Express & Star)

The Black Country Society

Founded 1967

The Black Country Society was started by Dr. John Fletcher who felt that the region did not receive proper recognition. The aim of the Society has been to foster interest and exchange of ideas regarding the past, present and future of the Black Country. It organises talks and walks on a regular basis and publishes a quarterly magazine: *"The Black Countryman"*. The author of this book has been proud to be a member of the society and was its President for one year.

The society has a website at www.blackcountrysociety.co.uk
and the editor of the Blackcountryman can be contacted at
editor@blackcountrysociety.co.uk

The right of Ned Williams to be identified as the author of this work has been asserted by him in accordance with the Copyrights, Designs and Patents Act of 1988. No part of this book may be may be reprinted or utilised in any form by any electronic or mechanical means without the permission of the author. Images used in this book come from a variety of sources and are duly acknowledged. Copyright rests with the original photographer. All photographs have been used without any intention of violating anyone's rights. If anyone's images have been used without the correct permissions, then apologies are offered and matters can be resolved in discussion with the author.

The Gornals: Volume Two
By Ned Williams
Published by Uralia Press
23 Westland Road, Wolverhampton, WV3 9NZ
Cover design: Geoff Tristram and Roger Crombleholme.

First published: November 2015
ISBN 978-1-898528-14-2

Printed by John Price Ltd.,
Bilston

CONTENTS

The Miners' Singing Quartet plus one! The gentleman second from the left is Jack Abbiss, later landlord at "The Swan". He was also choirmaster at the mission in The Straits – outside of which they seem to be standing.

Above: A splendid portrait of Sammy Jeavons standing outside the Ruiton Windmill in 1974, in his local costume, made for him by "Mr. Walker". Note the decorative sewing on the turn-ups, watch chain and fine silk scarf.
A few more pictures of Sammy Jeavons are to be found on pages 185 – 187.
(From the collection of Betty Caddick)

INTRODUCTION

Welcome to a second volume of photographs, information, memories and stories relating to The Gornals. When the first book, hereafter referred to as "Volume 1", was launched in November of 2014 it was greeted with much enthusiasm and immediately I felt that there was nothing for it – I would just have to carry on and produce a sequel! It is very easy for things to get left out of a first book – unfortunately that can continue, and it is quite possible that the fact about The Gornals that you consider to be the most important has still not be covered. That does not mean that I will be producing a third volume.

"Volume 1" was produced at great speed, following some initial prompting from Bill Caldwell and Brian Paton. Such speed was possible because I received so much enthusiastic help from everyone in The Gornals who offered help, but it also meant that production was fairly intense. Once again much help has been forthcoming but it has been difficult to maintain my response to the intense demands of book production. It is amazing that I now find myself presenting the second volume knowing that there are many people still waiting for me to pick their brains and consult their memories. I apologise for not managing to see everyone even if they found their way onto one of my many lists. This means two things: interest in The Gornals is alive and well, and secondly that a "furriner" has been allowed to continue the project.

In the introduction to "Volume 1" I outlined my gradual acquaintance with "The Gornals" – an exile from London gradually exploring the Black Country, firstly from a base in Dudley, then Wolverhampton. Having "caught up" with The Gornals, I can honestly say that The Gornals provide all that is wonderful about exploring the Black Country: friendly folk with tales to tell and even some photographs to share… I have spent over fifty years in The Black Country which has given me plenty of time to observe great changes and to approach the task of understanding what can make a Black Country community tick.

In The Gornals there is plenty of "ticking" still going on in the communities that make up the area but that has to be seen in the context of the changes occurring. Some of those changes might seem negative, others may be positive. At the time of writing (Autumn 2015) the bank in the centre of Gornal Wood appears to be about to close. Meanwhile the local library has been improved and we hear good news of the local Townswomen's Guild being re-born. Such day to day things add up to a mixed picture. Gornal does not currently celebrate being Gornal by holding an ambitious carnival but other initiatives have been tried – such as the "Community Service" at the Zoar Chapel, and the event being organised for December 2015 – coinciding with the launch of this book!

It has often seemed that The Gornals managed to preserve their individuality partly as a result of their comparative isolation – situated on the west flank of The Black Country and a little off the main arteries of the region. Many Gornal people worked within the area and each village does seem to have been fairly self-contained. All this created the "inter-relatedness" of life in The Gornals which soon becomes clear in these two books. However, the search for alternative work opportunities and the demand for access to better educational options gradually led the people of Gornal to overcome the isolation from the inter-war years onwards. There has also been quite an emigration from The Gornals over the years and many people have told me that copies of "Volume 1" have been despatched to relatives now living all over the world! Aynuk and Ayli may be still drinking in the same pub as their grandfathers, or attend the same chapel. Meanwhile their cousin might be digging for gold in Australia or running a bar in Thailand

The other "change" that is at work in The Gornals will be the number of "incomers". A long overview of this may be that such a dynamic created the character of The Gornals in the first place, but the immediate feeling maybe that there are many people now living in The Gornals who have yet to engage with the "inter-relatedness" of things that old-time Gornaliltes enjoy.

Alongside emigration and immigration is the fact that people with long memories of Gornal's past are passing away. Books like these try to capture what they can tell us before they have gone, and in this way try to contribute to the survival of a collective memory. I am reminded that in August 2015 Pearl Juliard died, but I had been fortunate in speaking to her while compiling "Volume 1" and her contributions were included in the book. Others leave us on a weekly basis and sometimes it seems that memories are disappearing faster than they can be collected. Many of us know that experience of not having asked enough questions of our late relatives! So – there is a lot of work to be done on recording the past, while making sure that we keep up with the excitement of the present – maybe a new shop opening in the area, or something fantastic going on at a local school.

Above: Compiling a book such as this involves looking at lots of pictures of people – many being of only immediate family interest. The task is to find pictures of wider interest, hopefully capturing a spirit of the time, or the individuality of a location. Here we see some Gornal folk – posing on the recreation ground just off Abbey Street in the heart of The Gornals in the early 1950s.
Back row: Bob Freeman, Graham Flavell, Allan Timmins, Ralph Simner, Mary Cashmore, Valerie Brettle.
Front row: Mike Capewell, Albert Price, Ron and Christine Stevens. (From the collection of Derek Haden)

Another thing worth commenting on is that while these books are being compiled views of the past and present can be constantly challenged. For example my own view of the comparative isolation of The Gornals is sometimes based on the fact that the local mains roads seem to graze the area rather than run directly into it – leaving the Gornals a little "off the map". Reading Angus Dunphy's book on the course of the river Smestow, I was struck by the mention of a map showing the Himley Road as part of a trunk route from Birmingham to Chester via Dudley. Perhaps The

Gornals have been closer to the outside world than I had imagined!

So whether you like The Gornals to be "on the map" or "off the map", whether you like to revel in the past, or plan the present and future, whether your interest is in homing pigeons or space age technology, I hope you will all feel there is something in The Gornals for you. My task has been to put something about The Gornals into yet another book – and to hope that everybody enjoys looking at it. Once again, it has to be admitted that this could not happen without a lot of help from a lot of local people – that's why there is quite a lengthy "acknowledgements" section on page 191. After two books it has to be admitted that there is still much that has been left out – but I have been driven by the wish to share what has been poured into this volume before the end of 2015. After all – I am only a furriner – someone "from the off" – I may need to rest after so much pleasure in exploring The Gornals".

Concerning the structure of this book: it is similar to "Volume 1" but also slightly different. "Volume 1" started with topographical chapters describing each of the five Gornal communities: Upper Gornal, Ruiton, Lower Gornal, Gornal Wood and The Straits. This has not been repeated, and nor have the maps be included. However, an "Around the Gornals" chapter has been included to provide an explorer's over-view of the area as he or she makes their way through the communities. Chapters are then devoted to some of the topics covered in "Volume 1" so that new relevant material can be included. A quick glance at page 3 will make all this clear. The final chapter tries to penetrate the heart of Gornal's story – the "inter-relatedness" of people and the criss-crossing of their lives. Even with such a chapter in each book

Below: Librarians celebrate £40,000 improvements to Gornal Wood Library in 2015.
Left: Jan Saxon (Snr. library assistant) and right: Sue Spandrzyk (library assistant). (E&S)

7

it is not possible to provide an "all and everybody" description of The Gornals and the folks that live there. The stories have to be seen as "representative", or as case-studies based on the information that people have shared with me.

When looking at The Gornals today it can sometimes be difficult to see the boundaries of the original villages. I therefore continue to recommend that people should look at the relevant maps published by Alan Godfrey, and available from Dudley Archives or good local bookshops.
These maps show the area as it was at about 1900 and, as a result of being reduced from large scale maps, show considerable detail. In 1900 the villages had undergone their Victorian expansion but not yet been overwhelmed by the house-building that has gone on throughout the twentieth century. It component of The Gornals there fore stands out clearly in its own right. The sheets you will need are 67.07 "Sedgley (SE), 67.11 ("Gornal

& Wrens Nest"), 67.10 ("Gornal Wood") and 67.14 ("Shut End & Tansey Green").

Another way of keeping up with revelations about the life and times of "The Gornals" is via the Internet. A Facebook page called "Broad is ow we speak" acts as a forum for people interested in The Gornals. If you wish to contact me regarding matters arising from this book, please do so via my website: www.nedwilliams.com

Writing "Volume 1" was very special for me as it was my fiftieth book about The Black Country. What is special for you is that here is yet another book about "The Gornals". I hope you enjoy it.

Ned Williams

(Autumn 2015)

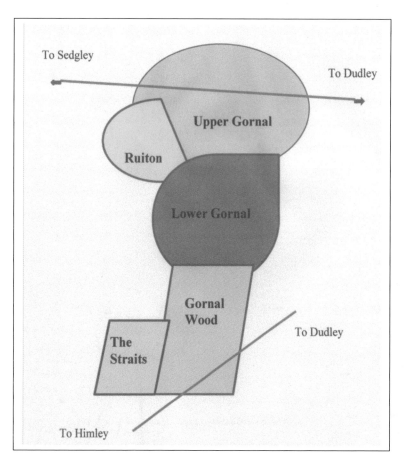

I have frequently been asked questions like "Where exactly are 'The Gornals'?" and I usually tell people they are a group of villages between Dudley and Sedgley on the west-facing slopes of the ridge that runs through the Black Country from Sedgley Beacon down through Dudley and on to the Rowley Hills. I often go on to use a sketch map like the one reproduced here, which starts with the Dudley-Sedgley road and the Dudley-Himley road and places the villages between those roads.

In the remaining pages of the Introduction I provide a few images that illustrate some of the main themes of this book, and show the variety of material that such a book has to include: everything that makes up a community – from pigs to politicians, from community groups to local institutions, from past to present.

Keeping abreast of changes in The Gornals:

Right and below: Keeping up with changes in the world of shopping is a challenge. There have been several changes since the publication of "Volume 1". Seen here is "Mr. Bumbles" – a new shop in Louise Street, Gornal Wood, which opened at Easter 2015. The shop specialises in the sale of "old fashioned" or traditional sweets, and replaces a hardware store. (NW)

A sense of community:

Maintaining a sense of community in the Gornals: Above: Alan Wedge addresses the members of the new Gornal Wood Branch of the Townswomen's Guild at its inaugural meeting on 16th September 2015 in the Darby & Joan club building. (Jo Robinson)

Left: Local school children are invited to lay crosses at the war memorial at Zoar Chapel, Gornal Wood in 2013 – on the day after Remembrance Sunday. (NW)

The Upper Gornal Pensioners Club is alive and well in its own premises in Clarence Street, Upper Gornal. Wednesday afternoons are popular Bingo sessions. "A Hymn, bingo and a cuppa seems a successful formula.

Right: Beneath a picture of St. Peter's church and a Degas print, Pat Thompson performs her duties as Bingo-caller, when not acting as Vice President.

Below: Members' concentration is intense during sessions. Note the hymn books neatly stacked after use during the opening hymn. (NW)

More about the history of this club is to be found on page 134.

The Gornals were administered, in local government terms, by the Sedgley Urban District Council, established in 1894, and there is an interesting story still waiting to be told of all the Gornal folk who served on this council, or aspired to be on the council but were never successful in being elected. Above: The last Sedgley UDC from 1965 to the end of March 1966 – when the authority was absorbed into an enlarged County Borough of Dudley. In the centre of the group is councillor Albert Turner – a Gornal man! (See "Volume 1" page 188.) Election material is to be found in a number of local family collections – like the examples seen below: Richard Jones was not successful in 1939, but Messrs Dews and Harris were successful in 1933. Fred Dews became the youngest chairman of Sedgley UDC. (Pictures from Diane & Terry Kinsella, Sue Windmill and Peter Handley)

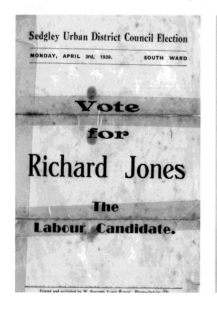

Since 1966 the Mayors of Dudley are invited to perform their mayoral duties in The Gornals, and of course, it is all the more significant if the Mayor is a Gornal person or a Gornal representative. Above: Councillor Alan Finch, from Gornal, performs the opening of the Upper Gornal Fun Day on 6th June 2013.
Below Left: Councillor David Stanley, of Gornal, in his robes while Mayor of Dudley during 2007 – 2008. His consort was Councillor Jill Nicholls.
David Stanley was first elected to Dudley Council in 1987, served until 1995 and was re-elected in 2000.

Far right: Councillor Margaret Aston, of Sedgley, helps launch "Volume 1" of "The Gornals" at Upper Gornal Methodist Church on 14th November 2014.Later in the book we see Margaret switching on the Upper Gornal Christmas Lights. Margaret has many Gornal links and has served on Dudley Council since 1995, becoming Mayor 2014 – 2015.

The world of local chapels and churches was one of the topics that dominated "Volume 1", and has continued to be a prolific stream of material. Above: Trevor Genge collected this magnificent image of the Chapel band at the Himley Road Wesleyan Methodist Chapel. Compare this with the pictures of the Lake Street band on pages 118 and 159 of "Volume 1". Chapel Sunday School anniversaries were well recorded photographically. Below: Once again Himley Road Chapel produces an excellent example.

Yet another subject that cannot be ignored in any study of The Gornals is the one-time presence of coal mining. We return to the topic of Baggeridge Colliery in this volume, while looking forward to the day when a definitive history of the pit is produced. Meanwhile, photographs like this appear – illustrating many different aspects of mining. *Right: Pictures of rescue teams appear like this from the early 1930s.* (Helen Birch).
Centre right: Pictures of men working underground seem rare, but in "Volume 1" (page 179) we were able to show Don Morris at work with a pit pony. In this volume we are able to provide pictures of Don when not at work. Here he takes his daughter Sue to Major's Farm. Left to right: Mr. Cartwright, Brenda Sharman, Jennifer Cooke, Young Major Jones, Geoff Jones (his son), Sue and Don Morris, Marilyn Matthews. Don and his pigeons appear on page 140.
Bottom right: Richard Jones on his 80th birthday at the Miners Welfare in 1969, with Jim Southall of the National Union of Miners. Richard Jones' NUM card is reproduced below and on page 12 we encounter him standing for election to the council.

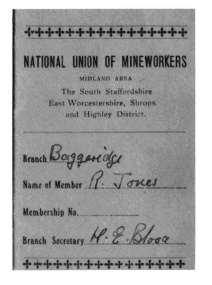

15

It has not been possible to compile a chapter on "Wartime Gornal", although this would be a worthwhile subject to investigate. I am indebted to Pat Wise who supplied these images of some Gornal folk on the Home Front. Above: The ARP/Civil Defence team photographed at Red Hall School. *Henry Wise, the Head Warden is sixth from the right in the middle row.* All the men and women seen here were recruited locally and several can be named. For example, Bill Fletcher, who kept the bicycle shop in Louise Street, is fourth from the right in the middle row. Sally Bate is third from the right in the front row – her family ran a grocery shop in Louise Street.

Far left: Lionel Guest in Civil Defence uniform. By day he was a brilliant electrician working at Gibbons.

Near left: Pat Wise appears here as a school girl. She attended Red Hall School and during the war displayed a yellow ribbon that indicated she could run home if there was an air raid. Mum in on the right, and the lady on the left is Mary Powney: Area Food Executive Officer.

In the chapter on "Sporting Gornal" you will see that this book follows a thread of sporting activity that begins in local school teams and progresses into local adult teams, for example those based at particular pubs. Some local sportsmen have progressed to professional teams.

Above: an example of a school team is seen here in the picture of the Red Hall School footballers, flanked by Andrew Barnett on the left and Michael Kinsella on the right. They are photographed on the Garden Walk football ground in 1955.
(Diane and Terry Kinsella)

A section on pigeon flying appears in a separate chapter – no account of Gornal life can ignore it but I'm not sure that the birds see it as "sport"? Here we see Sam Harris, his loft and his birds.
(Mary Jordan)

In both Gornal books, I have tried to avoid becoming involved in further endless enquiries into "Who put the pig on the wall...?"

However one cannot explore The Gornals without coming across people and their pigs. Three are illustrated here. There is also a nice picture of Jem and Hazel Evans and their pig-themed apple sauce boat on page 144.

Marsh & Baxter in Brierley Hill and Palethorpes, in Tipton, have made great use of pig images in their advertising, and the Bricklayers Arms in Kent Street enjoyed a brief existence as "The Pig on the Wall."

Top left: John Bayliss with his concrete garden pig.
Top right: Margaret Jeffs with her painting of the pig on the wall.
Left: Cathy and Phil Spencer with their pig – admired by many motorists passing through Gornal Wood on the Himley Road.

OPEN

Don't forget your Palethorpes.

Fresh sausages, pies, cooked meats and bacon. Palethorpes

18

The picture on the cover.

The picture on the cover of "Volume 1" featured a crowd of unidentified Gornalites outside Rounds Grocery Stores at Five Ways, Lower Gornal about 1910. The picture captures the excitement of an event in a small community but we lack more information. This volume's cover picture once again recalls the excitement of communal activity but in this case many of the people can be identified – and from this comes yet another lesson on the inter-relatedness of all things Gornal.

The picture comes from the collection of Rhona Pickerill and shows us a "concert party" group of people from St. James' Church between the wars. Members of the congregation worked together to put on entertainment for themselves, and the community. Such activities became even more ambitious after the opening of The Memorial Hall. Black Country communities once seemed bursting with musical and dramatic activity, plus sport and socialising in a wealth of contexts.

Back row: left: Sally Hewitt, Peter Woodall (father of Julian Woodall, who started the Scouts at St. James). The tall man, fifth from the left is Ernest Friend who played a significant part in the life of St. James' Church and is commemorated in a church window. He was a mining engineer and worked for Gibbons as well as fetching coal on his own account.) On the right is William Burrows the well-known printer who worked in the ex-chapel building on the corner of Humphrey Street and Lake Street. At the end is Evelyn Wise - wife of Harold Wise, the butcher in New Street, the Wise family also being much involved in the life of St. James. Front row, left, is Mrs. Moss who lived opposite St. James, and the lady with the wand is Edith Oakley, wife of Jeremiah Oakley. (Jeremiah had inherited his Christian name down the line from Jeremiah O'Leary whose story is told elsewhere in this book). (Edith became mother to the well known "Oakley Twins", David and John. (See "Vol. 1", page 196)

The Picture in the Vestry.

The two volumes on "The Gornals" reveal a community where a large number of people know each other, and might be related to each other. In such a community names are everything – even if it makes books like these rather complicated! Photographing and recording the names of everyone involved are complimentary tasks but we can easily end up with hundreds of photographs which future generations will be unable to identify. It is therefore interesting to study this "picture in the vestry" – a picture taken about 1930 of Sunday School teachers and/or bible study group members from Lake Street Chapel, Lower Gornal.

In 1994 Frank Littlewood (See "Volume 1" page 118) decided to record what he could remember about the people he recognised in the picture – a lesson in making a historic photo of value. With the help of Juliet Perkins, he numbered all thirty four of the people in the picture and wrote down what he knew, and related individuals to current members of the church's congregation!

In the space available we can give a sample of Frank's work. (Numbered from left to right, row by row.)

Back row: 1. James Bradley 2. Samuel Russon, 3. Richard Taylor 4. William Hickman 5. Thomas Hill 6. John Lucas 7. Joseph Evans 8. David Wakelam 9. James Beardsmore 10. Joseph Jones.

3rd row: 11. Violet Taylor 12. Polly Bradley 13. Jenny Bradley 14. Nellie Plant 15. Jane Timmins 16. Violet Bradley 17. May Cox 18. Maud Hale 19. Lil Massey 20. Alfred Greenaway.

2nd row: 21. William Jones, 22. Samuel Taylor 23. Alfred Jevons 24. W.T. Jones 25. Thomas Bradley 26. Isaac Taylor 27. John Hopkins 28 James Hyde .

Front row: 29. Isaac Taylor Jnr. 30. Isaac Bradley 31. Eli Beardsmore 32. Josiah Beardsmore 33. Samuel Bradley and 34. Daniel Taylor.

Frank added comments on all these people – ranging from comments on length of service in a particular role in the church, to simple observations about relationships. Who is doing such a job today?

Chapter 1
Around the Gornals

The first four chapters of "Volume 1" were devoted to a topographical tour of The Gornals, including diagramatic maps of each district. While there is no point in repeating this journey step by step in this volume, some readers may find it useful to mentally undertake such a tour to re-orientate themselves!

In "Volume 1" we suggested that one feels one has entered Upper Gornal from the Dudley direction once past "The Green Dragon", now an Asian Restaurant, so that is where our tour begins once again.

Right: The Green Dragon as it was in the early 1960s. (C.Brown)

Below: Recent steps taken to foster the identity of Upper Gornal have included the Annual Fun Day on the recreation ground, and switching on the Christmas Lights. The Mayor of Dudley, Councillor Margaret Aston, switches on the Upper Gornal Christmas Lights on 5th December 2014, on a stage erected in front of The Arcade. (NW)

Kent Street, Upper Gornal.

133-1.

The journey through Upper Gornal via Kent Street and Clarence Street provides many opportunities for considering how the landscape has changed. Above: This Edwardian Jon Price postcard shows Kent Street just beyond The Green Dragon – the loop in the tram tracks can be used to locate this precisely if you consult the "Alan Godfrey" map. (See comments in the Introduction.) Note the window cleaner at work on the new house on the left. (Olive Hyett Collection) Below: A 2014 view shows many of the houses seen above survive, but beyond Pale Street things have dramatically changed. (NW)

Top right: As can be seen in this contemporary view of Clarence Street, some buildings survive, others have disappeared. The former Shakespeare pub has become a Chinese food take-away but The Britannia is alive and well. In between, the old Upper Gornal branch of the Dudley Co-operative Society has gone and a new medical centre stands on the site. Pedestrian access still exists through to Club Row. (NW)

Centre right: "Volume 1" dealt with Pyott's shop and Spring House, once to be found at the top of Clarence Street (page 21), but this 1960s view shows Dave Hill's stationery shop on the site. (See page 35 of this volume.) (John Parker)

Below: Behind Clarence Street is the recreation ground, once partly quarried. The Ruiton Windmill still dominates the sky-line as the Upper Gornal Fun Day of 2014 gets underway on the site. At this point the boundary between Upper Gornal and Ruiton is rather blurred. (NW)

The windmill is very much the major surviving "icon" of Ruiton, located close to Vale Street which takes the explorer back behind Upper Gornal into the hamlet of Ruiton. The main part of the hamlet was to be found in the little streets off Hill Street – now substantially rebuilt.

Top left: The windmill forms the backdrop to this view of Harper's Quarry.
(Vilma Carter Collection)

Bottom left: Although derelict, the sails are still visible on this picture of the mill. It is currently the headquarters of the Dudley & District Radio Society, and is open to the public on the annual Upper Gornal Fun Days. Great views are to be had from the top of the mill.
(William Burrows)

Above: The Mill, in Windmill Street, seen from Hill Street at the time when the houses in the foreground had been cleared, wiping out the "feel" of old Ruiton. (Note Dudley's Eve Hill tower blocks on the horizon.)

Right: Below Vale Street, and the top of Holloway Street, are modern residential roads in the area where the ridge descended to Ellowes Hall. Looking towards Foxlands Drive, one can see one of the springs emerging from the ridge-side, feeding a stream that now flows into the Cotwall End valley.
Below: Volunteers clearing such a spring in 1968. (Alan Price)

Above: The chapel at Ruiton, Hermit Street, can be seen in the background of this view across one of the Holloway Street quarries. Sandstone was quarried for grinding into scouring material, and for work in furnaces. Several local families were involved: the Harpers, Waterfields, and Hydes.
(Author's Collection)

New houses are being built on either side of Holloway Street as the explorer descends from Ruiton down into Lower Gornal. The final ascent of Ruiton Street still retains a number of interesting buildings.

Left: On Five Ways itself are premises that were once "The Five Ways Stores", seen here in March 1989. (See "Volume 1" page 40.) John Thomas ran a general store in these premises for many years.
(NW)

Above: Five Ways, Lower Gornal, has been reasonably covered in a variety of photographs (See "Volume 1" pages 39 – 41, and page xx in this volume, but this picture taken by William Burrows of a 1950s Gornal Carnival seems to be the only picture to show Bunn's legendary fish and chip shop in the background! The parade is marching into Robert Street and when making comparisons with the location today one should take bearings from the building seen facing the camera on the left – which still exists, and whose story is told in "Volume 1" on pages 44/45.

Right: Similarly this picture of scouts assembling outside St. James' Church is interesting because looking across Church Street we have a rare view of "The Limes" on the corner of St. James' Street. The area occupied by the house is currently vacant. The scouts are described in more detail in a later chapter.)
(Mary Woodall)

The Humphrey Street area.

William Burrows took a number of photographs in the Humphrey Street area as it was his "home patch".

Left: Looking along a gas-lit Humphrey Street towards Lake Street, William Burrows captured an interesting view. The houses in Lake Street have survived, but a bungalow has been built on the corner.

Centre left: Dustbin Day in Humphrey Street. The elegant Edwardian house to be found in Humphrey Street is "Lyndhurst" – one time home to Gornal "names" like Alfred Allen and later Doctor Cunningham.

Below: Another remarkable William Burrows picture is taken from the wasteland in the "Graveyard" area looking towards Humphrey Street. It is just possible to make out The New Inn "The Sunshine" on the corner of North Street. (See "Volume 1" page 47.)

Above: The Swan Inn on the corner of Humphrey Street and Lake Street. Outside the pub are Florrie Abbiss and her son Derek. Florrie's husband was Jack Abbiss, licensee of The Swan, and one time organist at St. Andrews Church in The Straits, and once a member of "the Singing Miners" quartet. (Arthur Hale)

The descent in Gornal Wood via Church Street, Temple Street and Zoar Street has been adequately covered elsewhere so this time we take a detour into Redhall Road.

Right centre: the most famous building in Redhall Road was the Alexandra Cinema – known to everyone as "The Bump". (see "Volume 1" page 90.) It is commemorated today by Alexandra Court on the site. (NW)

Bottom right: Fan's Chinese takeaway at 16 Redhall Road was once Stan and Emma Bradley's shop. Stan took it over from Reg Brookes, and in his day it was the best fish and chips in the district! Another Red Hall Road legend! (NW)

HIGH CLASS PURVEYOR OF
FINEST QUALITY FISH

J. S. BRADLEY
Red Hall Road, Lower Gornal
FRESH FISH DAILY

All Customers Welcome
— Civility our Motto —

Above: Another of William Burrow's carnival pictures of the fifties provides us with a view of a shop front and street scene – this time in Temple Street.

Temple Street runs into Zoar Street and thence into the centre of Gornal Wood – the area known as "The Duckle". The betting office directly opposite the camera was once Dr. Cunningham's surgery.
(NW)

Left: The Abbey Road area is also well represented elsewhere. Here we pause to take in a view of the wool shop and TV/Radio shop overlooking "The Duckle" in the mid 1980s. The wool shop was being run by Jeremy & Hazel Evans. (See page 42.)
(Wilf Barratt)

A journey through Gornal Wood

These photographs by Janet Harvey, taken in 1960, take us through Gornal Wood in a remarkable traffic-free sequence.

Top right: Looking down Abbey Street towards Summer Lane. We can see the shop blind lowered over the butcher's window on the left. This was originally Bowyers shop, seen on pages 67 & 68 of "Volume 1" Turners Hill occupies the skyline.

Centre right: Everything seems quiet in "The Duckle", looking towards the Junction Inn and Louise Street.

Bottom right: Louise Street from the far end , looking back towards "The Duckle". On the left we can see Beddard's hardware shop. The sign advertisng Capstan cigarettes reminds us that Frederick Beddard was also a wholesale tobacconist.
(See" Volume 1" page 74.)

Above: Gornal Wood is left behind as we head down Straits Road past The Fiddler's Arms, rather hidden in this view out towards The Straits. (Janet Harvey)

Below: The colliers' houses in The Straits built in 1937, now surrounded by post-war housing. The National Coal Board disposed of them in 1971, after the closure of Baggeridge Pit. The photographer is standing outside 88 (now 81) and Is looking eastwards towards St. Andrew's Church and the house beyond which incorporated Mrs. Fellows' sweet shop. The picture was taken in 1947. (Gordon Tomlinson)

Chapter 2
Another look at the Shops

There was no specific chapter on "Shops" in "Volume 1" because they were described in the book's early chapters in which each community in the Gornals was described geographically. This time round a chapter is being devoted to the shops as several contributors have come along with photographs of shops and shop-keepers, or their accounts of particular businesses. As with the schools chapter and chapel chapter, they are arranged more or less in a progression from Upper Gornal down to Gornal Wood and out onto the Straits.

Right: Olive Hyett produced this "wrapper" from George Round's grocery store at Five Ways – a shop featured on the front cover of "Volume 1" and page 40. The wrapper includes a good portrait of the premises. The building survives today, in rebuilt form, and now includes a beauty shop.

The main road through Upper Gornal, starts as Kent Street and then becomes Clarence Street as it makes its way towards Sedgley. There were plenty of small shops along this stretch, most of which have now disappeared. Local retailing is now centred on "The Arcade". The latter is a late 1960s three-sided "shopping plaza", which originally included one or two retailers who had previously traded on the main road.

Right: Elizabeth Allen (nee Williams, born about 1844) stands outside her drapery shop at 28 Kent Street, Upper Gornal. The business had been run by her husband William but he died sometime in the 1900s and by the time of the 1911 Census Elizabeth is running it alone, and sharing the premises with her daughter Gertie, who gave piano lessons.
Her daughters Alice and Sarah had left home to become a school mistress and a photographer's assistant respectively.
Compare this picture with the one on page 16 of "Volume 1" (Olive Hyett – grand-daughter of Mrs. Allen.)

Above: The Arcade, Upper Gornal, 2013: a typical 1960s approach to "saving" the heart of a village. (NW)
Below: At 106 Kent Street, just beyond the present site of The Arcade, was the Upper Gornal Branch of the Dudley Co-operative Society. (See page 18 of "Volume 1".) This picture shows the "Guild Hall" built directly behind the Co-op. As well as being used by the Co-op, the premises could be hired as a "function room" and was used for wedding receptions. This is believed to be Freda Harris' wedding reception of 1943. (Mary Jordan)

Above: Dave Hill's shop at the top of Clarence Street. The shop was a newsagency and general toy and stationery shop. The building behind it was Tudor Joinery. (Compare this with the picture on page 21 of "Volume 1" when the premises were used by the Pyatt family. (John Parker)

Below: The Handyman Stores, 27/29 Clarence Street, Upper Gornal. At one time four cottages stood on the site of this store and the adjoining car park. Ken Jones bought them, demolished them about 1960, then opened the business – finally passing it on to new owners in January 2014. His daughter Kate still runs the cake shop at the rear of the car park. Note the proximity of the Jolly Crispin pub. (NW)

The shop in Hill Street.
This building had once been the home of Albert Edward Hartill – a carpenter. (A 1912 directory also lists him as owning a pawnbrokers shop in hill Street.) He had two daughters and a son – who grew up to become a Vicar of St. John's Church, Wolverhampton. One of the daughters ran this shop as a pawn shop and married a George Jones. They developed a business that survives in Wolverhampton today, selling electrical and gas appliances.

Left: The shop at 23 Vale Street, photographed in 1981 when it was selling antiques. For years it had been "Byfield's" and had been the place that many a broken radio or electrical appliance had been "fixed". The shop also re-charged accumulators. (Vilma Carter)

The shop that got away!

Emma Purshouse, and her mother Jennifer, wanted the book to include a picture of the family's shop but perversely the photograph disappeared. If we go ahead and include a mention of the shop the photo is bound to turn up the day after this book is published. *Left: Sarah and Harry Pugh, who ran a shop from their home at 36 Clarence Street. Harry was a moulder, but Sarah baked bread on the premises and their daughter, Emily, delivered it on foot. Emily was born in 1906 and was the youngest of twelve children. She worked at the shop until marriage in 1931.*

The Holloway Stores

The rather square building on the corner where Ruiton Street becomes Holloway Street is quite a prominent landmark. The building was erected by Bill Timmins after the War. John Fellows decided to lease the left hand part of the building, having already had some success in retailing a 1 Temple Street. (See below.) John was in the Fire Service, and eventually sold the business to two other firemen: Jack Baker and Charley Johnson. John Fellows also had a house in Holloway Street from which his wife operated a hairdressing business.

The other half of the building was originally occupied by Mary Dews, and it dealt with drapery and women's clothes, before becoming a hairdressers.

In recent years the grocery has been provided as part of the "Lifestyle" scheme, and for eight years the hairdressing salon, "Freak 2 Chic" has been run by Hayley Upton.

The advert (right) dates from 1961, and appeared in the St. James' Church magazine.

Shop at . . .

J. FELLOWS

HOLLOWAY STORES

Ruiton Street, Lower Gornal

for

G R O C E R I E S

F R O Z E N   F O O D S

C O N F E C T I O N E R Y

Keen Prices

Typhoo Tea 1/7 ¼lb. Corn Flakes 1/4½.

MANY OTHER BARGAINS

'Phone—Sedgley 3715

Phones : Sedgley 3009 & Dudley 54789

GEOFF. JOHNSON

HIGH-CLASS FAMILY
BUTCHER

LOWER GORNAL and

WEST BROMWICH

Above: Five Ways is the centre of Lower Gornal and has been served by a number of shops, including Rounds Stores featured at the beginning of this chapter and the shops along Ruiton Street. Here on the corner of Lake Street we can see that The Five Ways Inn has become the offices of A.R. Jones – a local funeral director. The little building next door is currently the Post Office but in "Volume 1" it can be seen in earlier guises – as the butcher's shop adjoining the pub and as Littlewood shop to the right. (Both on page 41 of "Volume 1". On page 40 a picture shows the former as a butcher's shop run by Geoff Johnson.) In trying to understand who Geoff Johnson was, one goes back, in true Gornal fashion, into the complexities of family history.

Geoff Johnson was the son of Agnes and James Johnson. He grew up in a shop they ran in Wellington Road, Dudley. Agnes was one of three daughters of John and Elizabeth Turner. Geoff took over the shop at Five Ways about 1938, taking over from his aunt Mary Cornmell – another daughter of John Turner.

Geoff went into The Forces during the war and then returned to Five Ways, later opening up a number of other shops. His son Robert, born 1940, later worked at Five Ways for few years before running a shop in Southalls Lane, then West Street, Dudley, from which he retired in 1999.

Below: An advert for Jarvis' shoe shop – once just around the corner in Robert Street. "G.H." was Gladys Honor Jarvis who shared the business with her sister Doris Irene who was better known as a teacher at Robert Street School. They had grown up in Robert Street, there father Thomas being a bootmaker.

You Get the BEST VALUE in FOOTWEAR — from

G. H. JARVIS

Boot and Shoe Dealers

92 ROBERT STREET — LOWER GORNAL

Agents for the Leading Makers including
PORTLAND, LIBERTY, FINN, TWO-STEPS, etc.

Whitehouse's Cycle Shop

No. 1 Temple Street has a long and interesting history. In the 1880s it was the home of Joseph Westwood – the first Headmaster of the Red Hall School. In the 1911 Census we can see the premises are being run as a grocery store by Harry and Minne Evans. Minnie Evans was there until 1946 when it was taken over by John Fellows (See page 37). From John Fellows it passed to Mr. & Mrs. Turner and they sold the shop to David Whitehouse in 1970.

David Whitehouse began by selling car accessories but gradually introduced cycle parts and moved on to selling the cycles themselves. Selling cycles really took off, and at one time the shop had about two hundred cycles in stock. Later still David started selling electric bikes and even diversified into key-cutting. (Hiram Price was one of the first people to try out the 15mph "Powerbike" – Hiram sold sweets from a nearby shop, and was a well-known evangelist.)

David retired in 2007 and the premises were sold to Bob Hopkins.

Right: David Whitehouse at the cycle shop.

Above: Bill Davies' Carpet Shop at 25 Zoar Street in 2014. It has since been rebuilt with a new shopfront. AT one time this was Alan Hickling's "snuff factory" (See "Volume 1", page 59), but it was later used by Hiram Price (See page 39) as a sweets and grocery shop. When Hiram was out making deliveries, the shop was run by his wife Florence.
(NW)

Below: Rene Evans Dress Shop at 8 Zoar Street, seen from the opposite point of view to the picture on page 61 in "Volume 1", although identified once again by the lowered blind. Rhona Pickerill ran the shop from 1962 to 1983, retaining its original name. Rhona was assisted by Marjory Walton, Mrs. Tennent, and later Joyce Price, selling women's and children's clothes. Rhona took over the dry-cleaning shop next door and that became a ladies' hairdresser. The picture, one of Share's postcards, also shows the Zoar Street approach to the centre of Gornal Wood, with the chapel on the skyline.
(Janet Harvey)

RENE EVANS

for

LATEST STYLES IN LADIES' MILLINERY, DRESSES, SUITS, Etc.

Baby Linen a Speciality

8, ZOAR STREET

Tel: Dudley 53053

Barclays Bank

In 1900 the United Counties Bank opened a branch in Gornal Wood in house-like premises at 12 Zoar Street (seen on the right). The United Counties bank was started in Birmingham way back in 1836. The Lower Gornal bank was a sub-branch to Dudley, and opened just two days a week.

In 1916 the bank was taken over by Barclays Bank, the United Counties being the second largest of a number of acquisitions made by Barclays – giving the latter a major presence in the Midlands.

The bank moved to a converted shop at 50 Zoar Street in 1958 – a year before becoming a "full branch" (centre right).

Finally on 10th January 1966 the new branch of Barclays Bank was opened in the present premises, at 51 Zoar Street – although these are currently threatened with closure. Barclays Bank started automating its branch accounting in 1961 and the Gornal Branch was linked to the new computer centre, near Manchester in 1972. The village's first "ATM" was installed at the bank in 1992.

The Bank also provided a sub branch at Upper Gornal from 1950 to 1989.

Bottom: Barclays Bank at 51 Zoar Street early in 2014 . (NW)

Above: This view looking up Zoar St. shows the branch of the bank in its 1958-1966 premises.
(Janet Harvey)

The Cosy Corner Café & the wool shop.

At some time during the Second World War, Ben and Annie Evans bought the premises at 12 Abbey Road, which became the family home and in which Annie ran a wool and general haberdashery shop.

At the rear of the shop was a low bric- built building which was opened about 1949 as the "Cosy Corner Café". Ben set this up with great enterprise and zeal and soon it was very successful and became an important part of the village scene, staffed by relatives and villagers. Up to a hundred lunches a day were sold at the café at one time – including meals provided to children who came in from Red Hall School – joined by some of the teachers. What was remarkable was the breadth of the "customer base" as it we would call it today. Villagers and school children were not the only customers welcome at "The Cosy Corner". Teenagers were welcome as well as motor-cyclists – the café being open till ten in the evening and seven days a week (2 till 5 on Sundays!). When the fairs were built up on the land by the British Legion all the fairground folk came down to the café. Ben Evans said that he was happy to cater for them all, without the prejudices sometimes prevalent at the time. If people complained about the café's popularity with young people, he would reply, "While there in my café, you can be assured they're not up to mischief!" He was a pioneer in installing a juke box and pin-tables. It was a café for everyone!

Ben ran the café until about 1961, and a year or two later the wool shop was leased to Dan and Margaret Gadd. Ben's son Jeremy and his wife Hazel, took over the wool shop, greatly expanding the range of goods on sale and stayed until 1989, after which it was occupied by Mr. Timms, the solicitor. More recently the shop has become a Chinese take-away. The one-time café building is no longer in use.

Top left: Lads outside the Cosy Café: Jack Brooks, Don Collins, Malcolm Russell, Robert Oakley, front row: Trevor Jones, Don Guest and Les Hickman. (Jem Evans)
Centre left: The building which once housed the Cosy Café as it is today. (NW)

Above: Motor cyclists outside the Cosy Corner Café in Gornal Wood in the sixties. Dennis Horton has been identified as being in the centre of the picture. (Bob Bradley)

Abbey Road, Gornal Wood

Right: Jeremy Evans took this photo from the room above his parents' wool shop, looking across "The Duckle" towards the Zoar Chapel and the White Chimneys pub, about 1985.

The row of shops forming this part of Gornal Wood can be seen "under construction" on page 8 of "Volume 1". Having been around for fifty years they now have a history and some premises have changed hands several times.

Centre right:
In this picture Family Fare is next door to E. Hodgetts & Son, the butchers, and the Star News Shop.
(Lynda Bridgwood)

Right: The Gornal Wood shops as seen in October 1982. Family Fare has become Cut Cost, and the butchers' shop is now being run by Keith Boxley where he is selling his "Gornal sauages". The Star News Shop has become "The Village Fisheries".
(Joanne Robinson collection)

The Changing Face of Louise Street

The "south side" of Louise Street is less photographed than the "north side" because it is less lit by the sun!
It also seemed to develop later than the "north side", home to so many locally well-known businesses. Sometimes changes to the street-scape are very subtle.
Top left: The Flower Shop on the corner of Bull Street and Louise Street is followed by a blank wall in this picture.

Centre left: In this 2015 picture, the cottage has been restored and turned into two apartments, and a new shop has been created in the space next door: "Best Wishes" – a card and gift shop. The corner position has been occupied by a florist for about thirty years, Julie Watton having run the shop for the past four years.
In "Best Wishes", Maureen Marsh and Julie Marsh have been selling cards since December 2012.

Below: Chesters has been owned by Robert Hickman for about 16 years, having previously been Horton's corn shop.
The men's hairdressers at "Top Cuts" has been run by David Dunn for about fifteen years. (NW)

Ladies' & Children's Wear

MEGAN

Stockists of

HARELLA
SALLY SLADE
BAIRNS WEAR

LOUISE ST., GORNAL WOOD

Louis Street – South Side

Above: Megan Turner's ladies-wear shop at 19 Louise Street. Megan opened the shop about 1946, it previously having been a draper's.

More information on Megan Turner on page 176.

Centre right: this aerial view, taken about 1985, shows Megan's shop has moved "next door" into No.21. this happened about 1955 when the building was new. She traded in these premises until about 2003, when she retired. From about 1958 until 1961 Jack Turner used 19 Louise Street to sell menswear and shoes.

Bottom right: A contemporary view of "Midway House" shows that "Lighting Majestic" now operates in No. 19 and the flower shop is now in No.21. Dave Cullis has traded as Lighting Majestic for about four years.

Top two photos: Jeremy Turner
Bottom picture: NW

Louise Street

Above: Round's cake shop at 40 Louise Street, with Greeta Cox and Lil Fox behind the counter, about 1973. (John Smith) The same shop today is illustrated below – as Mr. Bumble's Sweet Shop – home of traditional sweets from jars. (NW)

Centre left: Locally well-known names found in Louise Street have come and gone. This 1980s view includes The International Stores – heirs to George Mason's, Bassett's, Fletchers cycle shop and the Abbey Stores.

Bottom left: Shops change more frequently these days and it can be difficult to keep up!

Left: At Easter 2015 a new sweet shop opened in Louise Street, trading as "Mr. Bumbles", replacing the Village Garden & Hardware Shop. In the 1980s it was an estate agent (See "Volume 1" page 73), and before that it had been a bread and cake shop – first Griffiths' and then Round's, as seen above, and page 8. (NW)

Vanished Shops & Shop-keepers

Right: Benjamin Ball, born in 1892, the son of Richard Ball, a miner of Lake Street. He joined the grocery trade and dreamed of running his own shop. In 1920 he married Ethel Beardsmore, a tailoress of Brook Street (far right). A year or two later they took over the double-fronted shop at 36 New Street (See "Volume 1", page 83) next door to Wise's the butchers.
(Pauline Richards Collection)

Centre right: The fish and chip shop in Brookdale, on the right of this picture, became a drapery store run by Val Worwood about 1997.
Next door was Charles Watton's general store. The children are Donna, Delwyn and Dristan Worwood. (Val Worwood)

Below: One might be surprised to find that large late 1960s developments like the parade of shops in Park Road has completely vanished. It included Billy Hughes' fish and chip shop, and Mrs. Lawley's clothes shop.

The Shops in The Straits

Top left: Megs Store has been serving the people of The Straits for half a century. Originally it was operated by messrs Massey & Aston, then Roy Stevens, and then Daphne Jones. Since 15th July 1991 it has been run by Meg Love – who is now serving the children of her original customers. The Love family had once been licensees of local pubs such as The Wagon & Horses, The Limerick and The Crooked House. Meg was a lass from Pensnett who used to come over to Gornal Wood on the 137 bus – and met her future husband at the Cosy Corner Café – described on page 42.

Centre left: "Just for You", the florist, has become a dog-grooming parlour in recent times. In this 2009 photograph "News Express" has taken over the former Star News Shop and is being run by the Midland Co-operative Society. The shop included a branch post office. The Co-op disposed of the shop to the Life Style group and the post office closed early in 2015, but has since re-opened.

Below: The over-all view of the parade in the Straits in 2014.

Chapter 3
Church and Chapel

In "Volume 1" we looked at the churches and chapels of the Gornals by taking the three Anglican churches first, then the Roman Catholic Church, and then the Non-conformist chapels.

In this section we will look at additional information on these institutions but deal with them in "geographical order", starting in Upper Gornal, passing through Ruiton to Lower Gornal and then to Gornal Wood and the Straits. This provides a slightly different over-all picture, and of course, there is more additional information about some of the churches than others. For example St. James' was rather under-represented in "Volume 1", but more photographs have now come to light. (For keys dates etc., it is advisable to return to the account in "Volume 1".)

Below Left: The Cubs are seen turning from Clarence Street into St. Peter's while on parade in 1981. The Bricklayers Arms and the Green Dragon can be seen in the background.
Below Right: Emerging from St. Peter's.
(Vilma Carter)

Church and Chapels in Upper Gornal

St. Peters Church still dominates the townscape of central Upper Gornal, with its striking Gornal Stone exterior plainly visible to all users of the main Dudley-Sedgley road. The Upper Gormal Methodists stand back from the main road in their modern building, but regularly change their "Wayside Pulpit" message to attract folks passing by. The Pentacostal Church occupies the corner of Eve Lane and at the top of Jews Lane is a childcare centre that was once The Rehoboth Chapel. The old Mount Zion building and the Wesleyan Chapel are the ones that have disappeared.

We begin our tour of Upper Gornal at St. Peters.

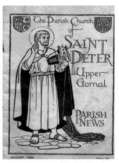

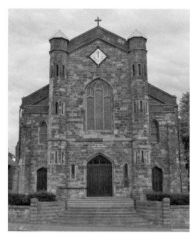

St. Peter's Church

Left: Scouts and Cubs at the altar of St. Peter's.
(Harold Raybould)

Left: The Parish Hall at St. Peter's was built in 1935 on the site of the National School building. One foundation stone was laid by the old scholars of that school and the other – see below – was laid by William Gibbons.

Bottom Left: The Christmas Fayre at St. Peter's makes good use of the Parish Hall on 29th November 2014. (NW)

Church and Chapels in Upper Gornal

Right: The Mount Zion Chapel in Clarnence Street eventually absorbed the congregation from the Wesleyan Chapel in Kent Street, and used this building until 1978.
(Trevor Genge Collection)

Right: The Mount Zion building opened in 1978.
Later the Wesley Hall was added to the back of the new church – seen in the background of this picture. Construction involved dealing with a spring on the site. Left to right: Helen Poole (Concord), ?, Rev Webster, John Bayliss, ?. (John Bayliss had worked for thirty years as a foreman bricklayer at Round Oak Steel works but when made redundant in 1982, trained as a Skills Centre instructor and led many MSC schemes such as this one.)
(Keith Bayliss Collection)

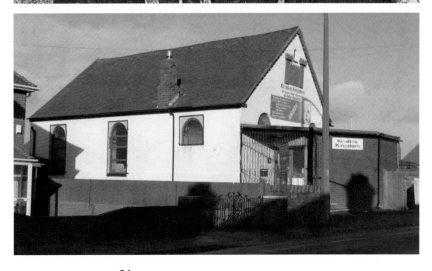

Right – The building seen here in 2014 as a childcare centre at the top of Jews Lane had once been the Rehoboth Chapel – described in more detail on page 112 of "Volume 1".

The Independent Chapel at Ruiton

Above: Boys and girls from the Ruiton Sunday School anniversary pose for a picture with Sunday School superintendent Bill Clarke. There had been a small sweet shop in Vale Street which opened on Sundays to sell sweets to the children attending Sunday School at Ruiton Chapel. Children tended to spend the money they were given to put on the plate and therefore Bill Clarke had to preach against such sinful ways.

Left: A Ruiton Anniversary – led by Choirmistress: Mary Fithern
(Vilma Carter)

Lake Street Methodist Chapel – Lower Gornal.

Left: Three members of the cast of "Joseph and His Brethren" performed by folks from Lake Street about 1930 to rasie funds for their new chapel.
Left to right: Tom Bradley, Isaac Taylor and Will Jones. All three were Sunday School teachers and later preachers, giving long service to this chapel. They also appear in the picture on page 20.
(Janice Maddox/ Vera Beardsmore Collection)

Churches and Chapels in Lower Gornal.

A Baptist chapel survives in Robert Street, two Methodist chapels currently survive in Lower Gornal – one in Ruiton Street, Five Ways, and the other in Lake Street. St. Paul's Protestant church is also to be found at Five Ways. (All described in "Volume 1")
Descending Church Street, we come to the Roman Catholic Church and the Anglican parish church of St. James'.

Top right: Five Ways Methodist church before being rebuilt in its present form. (See Volume 1, page 121.) (John Parker)

Centre right: A Five Ways Anniversary of the 1970s with Harry Pope as Sunday School Superintendent.

Below: A Five Ways Anniversary of 1985.
(Both pictures: Elaine Hyde)

Protestants and Catholics in Lower Gornal:

Left: the interior of St. Paul's Protestant Church, Five Ways, as it was in the 1920s.

Centre left: Structurally the interior of St. Paul's has little changed but the walls are now bright white and the pews have been replaced with blue-backed chairs – as seen in this 2014 view. (NW)

The exterior of the building is illustrated in "Volume 1".

Below: Views of the Roman Catholic Church of St. Peter and the English Martyrs, in its original form seem rare. (See Volume 1, page 107.) However , its distinctive exterior, or at least the porch, can be glimpsed in this wedding photograph of 1955 vintage. This was the wedding of Ron Walters and Rita Box, and, as can be seen in the group photograph, the wedding party lines up with the Church of England National School and Memorial Hall in the background.

Rita was the daughter of Bert Box, and Ron was well known because he worked at Bowyer's Butchers shop in Abbey Street.
(Rita Walters)

The parish church of Lower Gornal: The Church of St. James the Great

St. James' occupies a strategic site between the communities of Lower Gornal and Gornal Wood in the appropriately named Church Street. As one would expect of a parish church, it once played a significant part in the life of the community, and key members of that community played a key part in the church. More space has been given to showing this than was available in "Volume 1".

Right: This picture of the church is unusual in that it takes us back to a time at the end of the nineteenth century when the bell tower was topped with a steeple. The original building of 1817/19 had been altered in 1837, 1849 ,1863 and 1889 when the three-sided apse in the foreground was added.The bell in the bell tower came into use in 1909 but the tower itself was later declared unsafe for bell-ringing!

Below: The choir at St. James' – all male at the time – at St. James' about 1960. On the left hand side: Jim Bradley, John Jones, Ben Fullward with H. Blakeway and Jack Blakeway seated. Rev. Barlsey standing by the altar, seen behind Harold Horton, Graham Jeavons, with Brian Lavender carrying the banner. In front of them is Jim Boy, and on the right are Alan Twist, Don Collins, Peter Woodall and Bill Bradley.

St James' Church, Lower Gornal

Above: Processions used to play quite a part in the life of St. James'. In "Volume 1", the procession shown on page 98 was probably wrongly identified as a Confirmation event, it was more likely to be the Sunday School Anniversary as seen in this 1965 picture. (St. James' preferred to call it "the Young People's Festival" to distinguish it from Non-conformist practices!)
Alan Pickerill heads the procession, followed by the boat boy, and acolytes Jeremy Price and David Boyd. The crucifer is Leslie Hickman, and Brian Lavender is carrying the Sunday School banner. (David Boyd)
Below: The perfect setting for the Sunday School anniversary photo was outside the Memorial Hall. This occasion was in 1947 and shows the clergy, church wardens, servers and men and boys of the choir as well as the girls of the Sunday School. The vicar at the time was Father Shallcross, who left the parish later that year. A local street, on the site of the old vicarage, commemorates his name. (David Boyd)

St. James' Lower Gornal

Right: The Sunday School teachers at St. James' pose for a photograph between the Wars. Many come from families long associated with St. James' and its activities, and are related to the people we meet in Lower Gornal today.
Back row. Left to right: Ted Beardsmore, ?, Jeremiah Oakley, Lionel Bradley, ?, Tom Hayden, Peter Woodall, George Bunn. Middle row: ?, Mrs. Burrows, ?, ?, ?, ?, Alice Flavell, ?, Edith Burrows, Sally Hewitt (nee Oakley). Front row: ?, Nance Bradley (nee Oakley), ?, Mrs. Priest, ?, Ruth Hyde, ? .
(Lionel Bradley was the local postman.)
(Rhona Pickerill/Olive Hyett)

Centre: School pupils of the mid 1960s, or possibly girls taking their first communion, outside the Memorial Hall. On the right is William Bradley – a church warden and chorister. On the left is Sheila Pickerill, a Sunday School teacher.
(Rhona Pickerill)

Right: A Church of England Men's Society Branch was established at St. James' and they met regularly to hear visiting speakers, raise money or organise events at the Memorial Hall. On the left is Father Elliott, standing next to Jim Boyd. On the right is a vicar from South Carolina who had addressed the CEMS that night.
(David Boyd Collection)

St. James' Lower Gornal

*Between the Wars a successful "Concert Party" group was created at St. James – as illustrated on the cover of this book.
Left: In the late 1940s a Drama Group was established at St. James' by the curate, Rev. C.E. Lawson, with the aim of putting on plays with a Christian message. The name of the play presented by this cast is not recorded but the actors include: Standing: Alan Oakley, Aubrey Share, Ronald Marsh, ?, Celia Bate, ?, Lily Guest, William Sutton, Harold Blakeway, Jim Boyd, Rhona Bradley (later Pickerill), and Robert Cartwright.
Seated: ?, Megan Turner, Nancy Mansell, ?, and Donald Guest. (many of these folks had graduated from the Youth Club) (David Boyd Collection))*

Left: Members of the St James' Youth Club seen in May 1948 while on a trip to Weston Super Mare. (David Boyd)

Below: Members of the church, and the Youth Club returning from Blackpool Whitsun 1952. Third from right on the front row is Alan Twist who is still church organist today. Gladys Southall provided the photograph and she is third from the left in the middle row.

St James' Lower Gornal

Above: Boys and Girls of the Youth Club, 1948.
(David Boyd collection)

Right: Members of the St. James' church and Youth Club pose outside the distinctive frontage of the Memorial Hall in the late 1940s. The photo includes the Vicar, Father Shallcross on the right, and the Curate on the left. The Youth Club met two or three nights a week at the Memorial Hall.
(Rhona Pickerill Collection)

Right: A Sunday School anniversary/"Children's Festival" parade leaves the Memorial Hall for St. James' Church in the 1940s, led by Bob Timmins. The server behind him is Alan Pickerill. The Memorial Hall is another local landmark, and stands opposite the church as Church Street curves into Temple Street. It can be difficult today to imagine what a busy place this once was.
(Rhona Pickerill Collection)

The Memorial Hall, Lower Gornal   PN4318

The Memorial Hall

Some local people think of the Memorial Hall as a "village hall" but at its opening it was made clear that it was very much the "church hall", even if many villagers had contributed to its cost. In fact it was hoped that could be used as a Sunday School. Fund raising began in 1919 and the foundation stone was laid by the Bishop of Lichfield on 8th October 1924. It was designed by F.T. Beck and built by Messrs Gough of Wolverhampton at a cost of £5000. It was opened on Saturday 18th April 1925 by Lord Ednam and his wife. (It was their first visit to Lower Gornal!) Mr. Beck presented Lord Ednam with a silver key. The War Memorial was unveiled two years later.
Top left: The hall as illustrated on one of Share's local postcards.
Centre left: The interior of the hall today. (NW)

Bottom left: The "National School", later known as "The Mission House", built opposite the church at the top of Temple Street.

The Memorial Hall continued...

Above: Scouting was introduced at St. James' in the mid 1970s. (See later chapter). In this picture the scouts (in berets) and the cubs (in caps) pose on the steps of the Memorial Hall. The scouts eventually built their own scout hut behind the hall.
(Mary Woodall)

The Scouts and Guides joined other organisations within the church to take part in the annual Summer Fayre – the event seen taking place in these two pictures. In the lower picture Arnold and Olive Hyett can be seen manning their popular book stall.
(Mary Woodall)

SUNDAY SCHOOLS AND BIBLE CLASSES.

INFANTS — Morning 10 a.m., Afternoon 2 p m in Church
SUNDAY SCHOOL } JUNIORS — Mass 11 " Afternoon 2·30 „ in School
} SENIORS — Mass 11 „
MEN'S BIBLE CLASS ... Sundays, 3·0 p.m. in the Church
WOMEN'S BIBLE CLASS ... " " in the Memorial Hall
C.E.M.S. ... Second Tuesday in the month 8·0
MOTHERS' UNION Second Monday in the month 3·0
WEDNESDAY, GIRLS' SEWING PARTY, Parish Room. Juniors (under 14) 5·30; Seniors 7·30.
WEDNESDAY, SCOUTS at S. John's, 7·30. FRIDAY, GIRL GUIDES in the Memorial Hall, 7·45.

S. JAMES' (Lower Gornal) PAROCHIAL CHURCH COUNCIL
CHAIRMAN : The Vicar.
VICE-CHAIRMAN : Mr. Howard J. Jones.
CHURCHWARDENS & JOINT TREASURERS : Mr. H. J. Jones, Zoar Street
Mr. E. Beardsmore, Red Hall Road.
SECRETARY : Mr. S. F. Powney.
Rev. W. Edge Messrs S. Beardsmore, G. J. Bunn, W. Burrows, G. Gould, H. G. Marsh, A.W. Moss,
B. Oakley. Jer. Oakley, S F. Powney, S Price, J. Small, J. Southall, H. J. Sutton, N. Twist,
P. Woodall, Mesdames M. J. Hyde, S. H. Richards, Misses N. E V Burrows, D. E. Cooks.
ORGANIST : Miss Edith Hughes, The Vale, Ruiton.
ASSISTANT ORGANIST : Mr. John Raybould, Straits Road.
CHOIRMASTER : Mr. R. A Worton, The Mission House.
VERGER : Mr. David Waldron, 5 Humphrey Street.
SEXTON : Mr. Ambrose Guest, Church Street.

MAGAZINE DISTRIBUTORS.
Mrs. Bennett, Temple Street   Miss B. Corfield, Prospect Rd.   Miss H. Sadler, Summer Lane
„ J. Woodall, Parkes's Fold,   „ Fellows, Ruiton Street   „ A. Cartwright, North St,
„ Dixon, Sedgley.   „ Aston, Humphrey Street   Mrs. J. Fellows, Lake Street.
Miss G. Worton, Church Street.   „ B. Shaw, Boundary Hill.   „ J. W. Burrows, Humphrey Street,
Miss B. Astley, Musk Lane.   Mrs. J. Southall, Church Street

The Church Fete and the Bazaar

The annual church fete and "garden party" was once a major event in the church's calendar, up until the early 1930s. On 12th July 1950 a major attempt was made to revive the tradition, led by the vicar, Rev. Timms. The event was opened by Geoffrey Thomas, director of E & E.J. Pearson, the brick manufacturing company from Brierley Hill. (His wife was an active member of St. James' congregation.) Twelve year old Kathleen Bennett was crowned as Rose Queen. Such an event is illustrated on page 166 of "Volume 1". The fete had possibly been stopped in the early 30s to be replaced by a grand three day "bazaar" held in the autumn in the Memorial Hall.

Copies of the 1932 programme for that event seem to survive in local collections. Each day had its own grand official opening, starting on the first day with an opening by Mrs. Gibbons, wife of W.E. Gibbons.

St. James' Parish Magazine

The parish magazine produced by St. James' Church over the years can provide a valuable history of the church and its activities, and serve as a local "Who's Who". For example, a 1930 edition (top right) lists all the activities going on at the church from Sunday Schools to Mothers' Union and Girls' Sewing Group, as well as identifying everyone from the organist (Edith Hughes) and the choirmaster (Arthur Worton) to the magazine distributors. Howard Jones, local bank manager, church warden, and Vice Chairman of the PCC gets a mention – and is seen below – bottom left. He was also well known as producer of the shows put on between the wars.

From the archives we find pictures of the clergy – for example Rev. Harold Shallcross (below – second from left) and a picture of young Alan Oakley as Boat Boy about 1941. Bottom right: Alan can be seen as a server about 1955, carrying the banner at an anniversary. Maurice Woodall is carrying the cross and Nancy Oakley (nee Mansell) is on the right of the picture.)
(Alan Oakley)

Harold Jones, Rev. Harold Shawcross and Alan Oakley

Many Side-shows, Amusements and Games:—

FISHING FOR POP

PICK-POCKET

CROCKERY-MOCKERY

EGGS IN THE SAND

STOCKS

"BOWL THE VICAR OUT"

LUCKY STRAWS

BRAN TUB

A MUG'S GAME

COCONUT-SHY

PULL-A-STRING

BOUNCING THE BALLS

HANDKERCHIEF BLONDE

MOPPING THE CAN

GUESS THE WEIGHT OF THE JUBILEE CAKE

Teas
and
Refreshments
on Sale in
the Memorial Hall

THE JUBILEE RAFFLE
Prizes:
Piece of Cut Glass; Supper Set; Bottle of Whiskey, Gin, Sherry, Port and Wine; One Hundred Cigarettes and a Chicken.
Tickets — Price 5p. each.
Raffle will be drawn at the Garden Party.

★★★★★★★★★★ STAR ★ ATTRACTION ★★★★★★★★★★

SKY DIVERS

Will parachute into the Garden Party

at approximately 4.00 p.m.

Halfpenny Green Parachute Club

★★★★★★★★★★ STAR ★ ATTRACTION ★★★★★★★★★★

STAR ★ ATTRACTION   STAR ★ ATTRACTION

Ice Creams and Soft Drinks on Sale

Music by
ROBERTS SCHOOL
BAND

BALLOON
RACE

A VARIETY OF STALLS: —

RED, WHITE & BLUE

SWEETS

GREEN - FINGER'S

HOME-MADE

BOOK - WORM'S

CHURCH STALL

BUTTON - HOLES

SILVER JUBILEE BALLOONS

DRESSING - UP

For the Children:
PONY - RIDES

St James' Silver Jubilee Garden Party of 1977

One of the last really big events organised by St. James' Church was held to celebrate the Queen's Silver Jubilee in 1977. Father Elliot described it as an attempt to re-create an *"enjoyable 'get-together' such as our Village would have had in the old days on such an occasion."* With this aim in mind an ambitious garden party was arranged, and was opened by The Mayor of Dudley at 2.30.pm on 18th June 1977. As can be seen from the programme printed above, it culminated in sky-divers parachuting into the grounds! The church itself hosted a flower festival, the Memorial Hall hosted a an exhibition mounted Robert Street, Red Hall Middle, and Ellowes Hall Schools, and the Mission House was used for a display of craft work. At the time the church was running a Mothers Union, a Tuesday Ladies club, a playgroup and a "pram service" for mothers and babies, The CEMS, men and women's choirs and servers, Guides, Brownies, Cubs and Scouts.It seems surprising that no photographs of this event have surfaced for inclusion in this book.

1977
THE QUEEN'S SILVER JUBILEE
ST. JAMES THE GREAT, LOWER GORNAL
SILVER JUBILEE WEEKEND
18th and 19th June, 1977
Programme: Price 10p.

Right: Unidentified members of the choir at St. James' about 1960. The church had an exclusively male choir for many years. Note that in the 1930s church magazine "who's who", Arthur Worton is listed as the choirmaster (While living at The Mission House). Another well-known choirmaster, who had graduated from the ranks of the choir, was William Bradley - seen on page 57 – father of Rhona Pickerill who has supplied many of the photos of the life and times of St. James' Church.

Methodism in Gornal Wood

The early arrival of Methodism in Gornal Wood has been described in "Volume 1" (Pages 124/5 and 129), as described by William Davies in his little book of 1939. Eventually the Wesleyan Methodists built the surviving chapel in Himley Road, and the New Connexion Methodists occupied the existing site in Zoar Street – the third building on the site.

Left: The Zoar Chapel of 1906.

Centre Left: A Sunday School Anniversary at Zoar. Choir –mistress Gwen Brown stands next to the visiting preacher. The picture came from Mary Holmes who is standing third from the right in the back row on the lower platform. (Via Margaret Sargeant)

Below left: Double Wedding at the Zoar: John Payton marries Gwen Jones while John smith marries Olive Harris – on 14th October 1968. Both grooms worked for Baggeridge Brick Company. Olive was well known as bread van driver for Round's Bakery. Both girls worked for Round's at the time, but Gwen later worked in Woolworth's office in Dudley for many years. They walked to the wedding through a guard of honour provided by Clifford Williams' girls.

Below right: Frank Carter marrying Winnie Caswell, while the chapel boldly advertises the annual Harvest Festival.

Right: On 19th April 2015 the Zoar Chapel organised a "Community Service" to celebrate the community life of the Gornals

Top right: Rev. Steve Jackson, Rev. Jemimah Strain and Rev. Bill Cadlwell lead some symbolic paper-chain building as part of the "Community Service".

Centre Left: This view of the congregation assembling reveals the gallery and floor plan of the chapel from the minister's eye view. Both the Zoar and Himley Road chapels have large spaces available for worship and for community use and are well-located.

Below: Zoar's location can be used to good advantage on Remembrance Sunday as seen in this 2013 picture – the parade passes three non-conformist churches, the Roman Catholic Church and the parish church of St. James'.

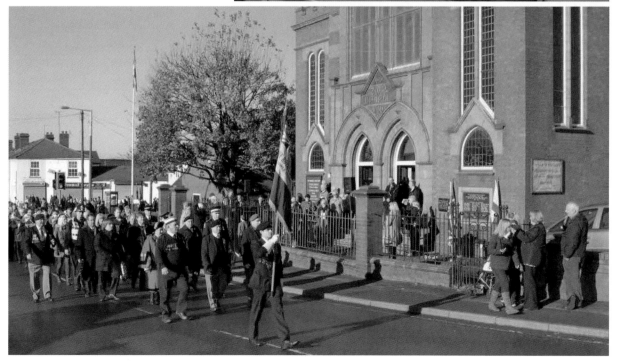

Himley Road Methodists, Gornal Wood.

Top leftt: The 1959 Sunday School Anniversary with Rev. Perry Smith occupying centre stage.

Centre left: The 1956 Sunday School Anniversary with Rev. Hunt in the pulpit.

Below left: A contrasting view of about 2008, organised by Kate Jackson and Karen Cartwright.
(Michael Buxton)

Himley Road Methodist Chapel, Gornal Wood

Top right: Usually the Sunday School pupils were photographed on the anniversary when seated on the "platform" but this time – at Himley Road – they seem to have been snapped outside the Sunday School. (Olwen Hough/Janet Harvey)

Centre right: One of a series of photographs taken of the Ladies' Bible Class at Himley Road. This one was taken in the 1930s and includes a portrait of William Davies – the Bible Class teacher. (Olwen Hough)

Bottom Right: Margaret and Michael Buxton receive a peace plaque from Bert Bissell at Himley Road. (Mike Buxton)

Saint Andrew's Church, The Straits

As described in "Volume 1", the Church of England established a small mission and school out in The Straits possibly as early as the 1830s. (It was regarded as "mission" of All Saints Church, Sedgley.)

The building began to collapse in 1905 as a result of the proximity of the coal workings and was replaced with a new building on the other side of the road. The new church opened in May 1914.

Top left: The 1914 church building as built – the view of the end wall now being obscured by the new church hall added in the 1960s. (From a picture collected by Wilf Barratt)

Centre left: St. Andrew's Church was able to celebrate the centenary of this building in June 2014. Eugenie Rhodes and her sister Irene played a part in putting on a display to mark this centenary. (NW).

Below: The Bishop of Dudley joined the choir and congregation of St. Andrew's on Patronal Sunday on 1st December 2014 Guest of honour on the day was the oldest member of the congregation – Maisie Glover, whom many people remember as a dinner lady at the Straits School.
(NW)

Chapter 4
Another look at Schools

Schools in the Gornals

"National" schools were built alongside the Anglican parish churches of St. Peter's in Upper Gornal, and St. James' in Lower Gornal soon after the churches were built. The local School Board, established by the 1870 Education Act, provided three schools: Red Hall (1880), Upper Gornal (1883), and Robert Street (1894). Further details are set out in "Volume 1".

Upper Gornal Board Schools

Above: Upper Gornal's "Board Schools" have disappeared, but for many years this building was a familiar landmark on Clarence Street. At the end of its life the building was known as the Tudor Schools, but old names stick and most people still talk of the "Board School" when referring to it. Below: This building was added, on the other side of the road, when raising the school leaving age led to the need for technical and domestic science rooms.

Upper Gornal Board Schools

Left: The building on the "Quarry side" of Clarence Street was eventually used as a youth club, but was finally demolished about 1987. Just before demolition this artwork appeared in the boarded-up windows, celebrating local legends. (Picture supplied by Vilma Carter, who attended the Board Schools, as did her mother and her sons.)

Centre left: A nativity play presented by the infants at the Board Schools. The Virgin Mary was played by Jean Davies, who also supplied the doll to play the baby Jesus (she still has the doll today!). The girl on the right is Maureen Flavell, and her brother Robert is seen carrying an urn on his shoulder. (Gary Westwood)

Below: Some Board School mixed juniors pose for a photograph in 1937 – Coronation Year. The children include Joan Green, Billy Green, Bill Sutton and Olive Mason. (Margaret Sargeant)

Upper Gornal Board Schools

Right: Upper Gornal Board School About 1931. The teacher is Mr Nott (on page 135 of "Volume 1" he appears in a picture of similar vintage but is unidentified!}. Arthur Byfield is sitting 3rd from left, front row. Reg Westwood is 3rd from left 2nd row from the back.

Centre right: Probably from 1934. Reg Westwood is middle row 5th from the right, the lad in the centre of the back row with the fringe is Arthur Byfield, he later had a shop in Vale Street next to the Good Intent where he repaired radios and later on TVs. He also charged the accumulators with which many people powered their radios. The lad sitting on the left front row is Joseph Harper who became the owner of Harper's quarry in the Holloway, Upper Gornal. The teacher has not been named

Below: A 1923 picture featuring many of the same boys. The teacher is Reg Price, whose son later taught at the school. (All three pictures: Gary Westwood)

Upper Gornal Board Schools.

Top Left: the 1933 football team with Mr. Nott on the left and the headmaster, Mr. Potts, on the right. (Compare this picture with the one on page 135 of "Volume 1".)

Centre left: The Senior Boys team in 1934. Mr. Potts is seen once again on the right, but the teacher on the left has not been identified.

Below: The top infants (Group 1). The school had opened with "Mixed Infants" and had originally segregated the sexes from the age of seven onwards. In later years, while operating as a primary school, all classes were mixed.

(All three pictures from Olive Hyett)

The Tudor School, Upper Gornal.

About 1958 the Board Schools were re-named "The Tudor School"

Right: School staff in 1981: Miss Dean, Mrs Wedge, Mr. Vian, Mrs. Thompson, Mrs. Haywood. Seated: Miss Pole, Mr. Duggan, Mr. Greenhalgh and Mrs. Harbridge, who lived nearby – in Vale Street.
(Vilma Carter)

Centre right: Parents outside The Tudor School about 1983 – protesting about the proposed closure. (Vilma Carter)

Crossing Patrols

Below left: The Tudor School crossing patrolman. (Jim Watton)

Below Right: Crossing patrolman Austin Hickman (1900 – 1978) worked at Baggeridge Colliery over fifty years in the Lamp House. When he retired he became a School Crossing Patrolman at the High Arcal School – where he is seen with his wife Mary. (They lived in Valley Road) He was a life-long Wolves Supporter and great supporter of miners' welfare – a socialist and strong union man. (Val Haywood)

Robert Street Primary School

Left: The modern entrance to the Robert Street School is part of the complex opened by the Duke of York in 2002: quite a contrast with the elegant Board School building of 1894 illustrated on page 137 of "Volume 1".

Centre Left: The demolition of the old school building in 2001 led Jesse Witton, nee Steele, to provide this school photo of 1932 vintage to the Black Country Bugle. She was unable to name any pupils other than herself, second from left in the second row.

Below: Margaret Jeffs, nee Haden has supplied this 1954 photo and identified some of the pupils including herself (second from left on front row), Denise Briscoe, Irene Turner, Georgina Jacovic, Johnny Whitehouse, Graham Jeffs, Tony Ball, Glynis Friend, Robert Greenaway and Pat Hebblethwaite.

Robert Street School

Above: The school was once well known for its choir, which won a number of festivals. The choir was directed by the headmaster, Arthur Worton, seen behind the left-hand shield in this 1932 photograph. He was constantly "talent spotting" at his school, and also recruited songsters to the choir at St. James' Church where he was choirmaster.

Centre right and lower right: Robert Street Primary School presented its work at an "open day" in 1959 and these two photographs capture the spirit of that time. Gymnastics are demonstrated in the school playground, followed by a display of Country Dancing.

(All pictures from the School's archives.)

Robert Street Primary School

In 1994 the headmaster, John Crighton, organised a grand centenary event.

Left: Here his seen with his teaching staff all dressed in Victorian costume for the occasion.

Centre left: The lunchtime staff also participated in the 1994 centenary celebrations by dressing in Victorian dress.

Bottom left:
Pupils also dressed in the Victorian style to celebrate the school's 1994 centenary and recreated street games in the school playground.

On the opposite page:
Two classroom photographs taken in the 1994 Centenary Year:
Top: The Reception "blue" class.
Bottom: The "red" class.

(All photographs from the school's archive.)

Robert Street Primary School

Top left: School teaching staff in 1987.
Left to right: back row: Judith Hall, Sue Royal, Jes Greenhough, Janet Brownhill, Alison Pearson, Margaret Harbridge and Penny Chisholm. Front row: Alma Bowen, Justin ?, Colin Bickley (Deputy Head), John Crighton (Head Teacher), Eva Fellows, ?, and Joy Wheeler.

Centre Left: Alma Bowen with her Infants class in July 1996 – the year of Alma's retirement.

(Both pictures from Alma Bowen's Collection)

Bottom left: The school's Millennium football team.

Note: Although we have referred to the school as Robert Street Primary School, it is now known simply as Roberts Primary School.

Robert Street School

Parents and pupils enjoy a Chirstmas Party at Robert Street School, sometime in the 1950s.

These photographs were among nine found in a skip, so dating the event and identifying folks has been difficult!

Above: The lady second from left is Mary Greenaway, fifth from left is the teacher, Mrs. Jarvis. (See page 139 of "Volume 1".) Third from the right is Councillor Joe Kendall.

Right: Among the ladies photographed at this event was Jean Middleton – in the patterned dress.

Bottom right: Activities included the traditional Gornal folk dance in which participants dance with a ball between their knees while holding a brolly.

(From the collection of Olive Hyett.)

Naming Robert Street scholars

Before leaving Robert Street let us once again return to the problems of identifying everyone in such pictures. In the above picture the teacher has been named as Miss Gwithers. Back row: Paul Amphlett, David Beech, Peter Lane, Graham Williams, Elaine Smart, Anthony Price, Raynor Burrows, Gerald Greenaway, Susan Tighe, Johnny Cook, Anthony Millward, David Parkes, Michael Hunt (standing alone). Front row: Betty Rowe, Stella Cox, Pat Fellows, Sandra Bullock, Johnny Green, ?, Linda Horn, Brian Bradley, Michael Fellows, Mabel Screen, Ronnie Thomas, Michael Timmins, ?, David Brownshill, David Gennard, Jennifer Willis, Ralph Hyde, ?, Tony Shuker, Sheila Thomas or maybe Esme Horton, Trevor Stanley, Glennis Jones.

By way of contrast, in the photograph on the left, only one person has been identified! The girl with a handkerchief tied round her arm, second from right, second row, is Kathleen Millicent Hickman, known to her classmates as Millie. She became the mother of Peter Lane seen in the above picture! (Peter Lane)

Red Hall Schools

The Red Hall Schools in Gornal Wood survive in the original Board School buildings – much as the school would love to be on one site rather than divided by a busy road! In the normal way in which the Board Schools developed, this school opened in stages and use of the buildings changed over the years. In condensing this history in "Volume 1", some misleading statements were made so please refer to the amendments listed on page xx. Such a history also creates the possibility of celebrating at least two centenaries – which the school did in great style in 1980 and 1991. Further photographs of these events follow in this section.

It is not possible to descend Zoar Street without admiring the Victorian splendour of these buildings. Bottom left is the elegant caretaker's lodge. Above we see the rear view of the building currently used by the juniors. Below right, as we look along the side of what became the "infants school", we can see the impact of adding more modern buildings over the years – "Teaching Block B" being in a less ornate style.

Red Hall School

To add to the world of infants, juniors, senior girls etc... let's not forget the nursery classes! Here is the nursery in 1974. (Kath Baker)

Centre left: "Senior Girls" – a cookery class, late 1950s. Mary Jordan, Mrs. Whitehouse, Joyce Price, Jean Witton, and Irene Guy, in their self-made smocks, making Yorkshire puddings. (Mary Jordan)

Below: A Junior School picture from 1950: Back row: Judith Southall, Eileen Spencer, Jean Bradley, ?, Browen Taylor, Trevor Shaw, Rosemary Horton, Sandra Taylor, Jennifer Timms, Barbara Whitworth, ?, Pam Marsh. Third row: Terry Evans. ?, Bobby Flavell, Brian Johnson, Melvyn Marston, ?, ?, Trevor Smith, Ronnie Flavell, ?. Second row: ?, John Flavell, Lol Stevens, Ralph Cartwright, ?, John Moss, Arthur Bate, Vincent Flavell, Jimmy Fellows, ?. Front row: Hetty Scott, Irene Flavell, Val Morgan, Janet Brooks, Dorothy Hale, ?, Nellie Fellows. (From Jim Fellows' collection)

Red Hall School

Right: Teaching Staff in 1955: Back row: Mr. Coates, Michael Kinsella, Arthur Baker. Front row: Miss Blackham, Mary Nicholls (Deputy Head), Mr. Evans (Head), Mr. Powell and Nora Harrison.

Centre right: Teaching staff in 1956: Back row: Arthur Baker, Michael Kinsella, Mr. Powell, ?. Front row: Miss Blackham, Andrew Barnett (Head) and Nora Harrison. This picture marks the arrival of Andrew Barnett as headmaster. His story is told in "Volume 1" – page 193.

Bottom right: A Red Hall School pantomime of about 1952, which is believed to have also been presented at the Memorial Hall.

Below: Michael Kinsella (1917 – 1993) taught at Red Hall School from about 1950, went on to Maidensbridge School as Deputy Head, then Lawnswood as Head, retiring in the early 80s. He was also associated with Robert Street Youth Club and was a local councillor and magistrate.
(Diane & Terry Kinsella)

Red Hall School

Top left: The Mayor of Dudley, on the left, with Julie Fellows - prize winner in an art competition, plus Tina Smith, who had won second prize. (Vivian Smith)

Centre left: Mirs. Mondon's Class 3, about 1975. Mrs. Mondon has been remembered for her story-telling skills! (Michael Buxton)

The cast of the Red Hall Middle School production of Red Riding Hood, presented in 1978. Leadin parts were played by Jennifer Crowe, Ian Jones, Alec Turner, Martin Hollis, Adrian Bentley, Gary Hawkins, Denise Hill, Andrew Nock, Beverley Tope, Karen Parker, and Suzy Johnson. It was produced by Wendy Hughes. (Joanne Robinson)

Red Hall Primary School

In 1980 David Eades, the head-teacher, led the school in celebrating its centenary.
One part of the celebrations was a carnival-like parade around Lower Gornal and Gornal Wood in which participants dressed in the styles of each decade of the school's existence.

Top right: Five Red Hall pupils dressed as soldiers: John Haney, Simon Smith, Mark Flavell, David Hall and Paul Hollis.
(Vivian Smith)

Right: A large number of parents took part in this parade. Some photographs, showing a glimpse of the locations as well as the particpants.
Bottom left: Kerry take spart in the 1991 celebrations.

(Olive Hyett: Centre and bottom right.
John Smith/Terrence Abbiss: Bottom left.)

Red Hall Primary School

The 1991 Centenary Celebrations.

Above: The School Centenary Parade passes from Zoar Street into Temple Street.
Left: Mary Abbiss, in 1940s suit and a wig, stands outside Whitehouse's cycle shop (see page 39).

Below: One of the murals prepared by Paula Wolf for the 1891 Centenary Celebrations.

(All pictures Terrence Abbiss)

Red Hall Primary School.

The 1980 and 1991 centenaries were not the only occasions celebrated in a very public way in the Gornals. When Miss Isobel Baugh retired as Head of the Infants School (then a "First School") in 1996 after twenty eight years at the school, it was celebrated over several days, starting with a social at the Baggeridge Miners Social Club, where she was presented with a rocking chair. On the next day she toured the area in an open landau, escorted by David Eades, and on the day after that she travelled by white Cadillac to another reception!

Top right: Crowds fill "The Duckle" (central Gornal Wood) as the open landau comes into view.

Centre Right: Isobel Baugh and David Eades smile and wave to the crowds as the landau passes the Zoar Chapel.

Bottom right: Mothers and pupils gather on the Recreation Ground to greet Miss Baugh after her tour.

(All three photographs: Joanne Robinson)

Straits Primary School

The school in the Straits opened in 1964, but at first with only accommodation for the infants. It was January 1968 when the completed site was opened by Alderman Wilson. Like the other local schools, its history is complicated by changes to the site and changes in structure, "Infants and Juniors", then "First and Middle", and then combining again as "Primary".

Above and left: Straits School today – a product of expansion and change.

Bottom left: Teaching Staff at the Straits in 1981: Standing: Mrs. Hipkins, ?, Mrs. Clark, Mrs. Plant
Seated: Mrs. Tredwell, Mrs. Price, Mrs. Dovey (Head teacher), Mrs. Skilbeck (Deputy), and Mrs. Walsh.
(Mary Clark)

(Edna Dovey was an ex - Dudley Girls High School scholar who had trained at Dudley Training College (1944-46). She became Head of "Straits First School" in September 1973. Faith Skilbeck was also ex- DGHS and teacher-trained in Dudley, and came to the Straits in September 1980.)

The Straits Primary School

In "Volume 1" a list of head-teachers at The Straits" omitted Adrian Slack from the list! He arrived in 1997 and stayed at the school for fifteen years, and is seen above with pupils celebrating the school's achievements. In the mid - 1990s the school had struggled to maintain numbers and satisfy inspectors, but Adrian and his staff were able to "turn the school round" in a creative way – thus reviving its fortunes.

(All photographs from the school archives.)

Above: Pupils celebrate the schools progress in the 2000s.
Below: The school hall at The Straits Primary School became a skating rink towards the end of a school project on "ice worlds" about 2000. Head teacher, Adrian Slack, takes to the ice on the right.

Ellowes Hall Sports College

The Ellowes Hall Sports College that we know today has grown out of the first major attempt to create purpose built secondary education facilities in the Gornals. Up until the mid-1960s, secondary education was provided for boys at Robert Street, and for girls at Red Hall. The one time site of Ellowes Hall itself (see below) was cleared and in the Spring of 1966 a brand new Ellowes Hall Secondary School opened – just as the Gornals became part of the enlarged borough of Dudley. A decade later it acquired full "comprehensive" status, and in the 21st Century, its present Head-Teacher, Andrew Griffiths (left) has steered its progress to become a prestigious "Sports College".

Ellowes Hall.

This hall was demolished and the surrounding site cleared to make way for the new school. In fact re-landscaping the former grounds of the hall continued after the school's opening and resulted in major changes to the terrain of this area.

Left: Ellowes Hall. (See page 55 of "Volume 1"

(Vilma Carter's collection)

Ellowes Hall Sports College

For a school that has become a Sports College it is interesting to note that the search for school photos has mainly produced pictures of sports teams of various vintage.

Top and centre right: Cricket and Football teams of the same vintage. Mr. Richardson (Headmaster) and Mr. Houston (P.E. teacher) are seen on the left and right of both pictures.

Bottom right:
The Head-teacher, seen on the left of the picture is G.W. Firth, who took the school into Comprehensive status in1974. He was Head from 1971 to 1981. The teacher in a tracksuit on the right of all three photos is Mr. J.B. Houston

(Pictures supplied by Jim Watton)

Below: The school badge used in the early days of the school. Compare this with the present badge illustrated on page 152 of "Volume 1"

Ellowes Hall Sports College

Top left: Ellowes Hall footballers

Centre Left: The Ellowes School footballers of 1967.
Left to right: Mr. Richardson (Headmaster), Steve Greenaway, Brent Wills, Phillip Green, David Ashley, Raymond Cooper, Keith Bayliss, Mr. Brind Robin Carter, Tony Ball, Ian Hollis, Gary Cox, Ian Waugh Gary Marson and John Smith (who later played for Dudley Town) Many later played in other teams – eg pub teams (See the chapter on Sport.) The teacher on the right is Mr. Brind.

Photographs: Keith Bayliss

Bottom left: Class photos of pupils at the Ellowes Hall School must exist in many Gornal homes, but this is the only one submitted for use in this book! Here is a class of 1984 vintage.
(Vivian Smith)

Ellows Hall Sports College

Right: The School canteen staff in the late 1960s. Standing:Third from left: Pat Millward,6th and 7th from left: Rene Jones and Kath Green. Front row: 2nd from left: Florence Owen, 4th from left: Mrs. Tibbs, the Supervisor, 5th from left: Jeanette Bayliss.
(Keith Bayliss)

Centre right: Ellowes Hall canteen staff on a night out: Letf to right: Renee Jones, Olive Witton, Jeanette Bayliss, Florrie Owen, Emmie Brookes, and Miriam Smith.
(Keith Bayliss)

Bottom right: The Ellowes School Lunchtime Supervisors of 2005, known as "The Redcoats". Left to right back row: Margaret Jeffs & Jill Hayes. Front row: Janet Cox, Liz ?,, Loraine Peters, Irene Elwell, and Shraon Bradley (current manager of the team)
(Margaret Jeffs)

A "panorama" photograph of everyone at the Ellowes School was taken in 1969. The only way to reproduce it in a book of this nature is to divide the picture into four sections and apologise for not naming every pupil! Staff from, left to right, have been identified as: ?(Assistant caretaker), Mr. Rogers (Caretaker), Mr. Salmon, Mr. Davis, Mr. Emery, Mr. Hopkins, Mr. Barnes, Mr. Kelly, Mr. Hipwell, Mr. Child, Mr. Davies, Mr. Tromans, Mr. Sayers, Mr. Chance, Mr. Lockner. And then continued on next page:

George Pearson (Head of Lower School), Mr. Neil (Deputy Head), Mr. Richardson (Head), Miss Bissell (Deputy), Miss Jones, Mr. Whitehouse, Mrs. Dews, Miss Morris, ?, Miss Monk, Mrs. Powell, ?, Mrs. Dudley, ?, Miss Downing, Mrs. Gibbons, Miss Salmon, Mrs Smith (Head's secretary), her assistant, Mr. Harris (Head of Lower School). Next to Mr. Harris is Karen, the Head Girl, who later married David Smith (the Head Boy) who is seen next to the caretaking staff at the other end of the staff.

The Ellowes School Photo of 1969 Continued.

Above – the right hand sections of the "panorama", taken on the school tennis courts in 1969.

Right: The Senior staff of the school, as they appear in this 1969 "panorama" of the complete school, are seen more clearly in this enlargement. Mr. Richardson, the school's first head teacher is seated second from the lett. (He came from Scotland and enjoyed the nick-name, "Batman"!) His deputy, Mr. Neil, on the left, came from Robert Street Senior Boys, and his other deputy, Miss Bissell third from the left, came from Red Hall Senior Girls. On the far right is Miss Jones, the school librarian.
(Jim Watton provided help in using this "panorama".)

Ellowes Hall Sports College

Over the years the Ellowes Hall School has gained a high reputation for the scale and quality of its musical drama productions.

In November 2014 the school presented a large scale production of "Les Miserables".

Left: Headmaster. Mr. Griffiths, joins some of the cast of "Les Miserables" during the interval.

Centre Left: Some of the cast of "Les Miserables" in full song.

Below: The school's success in music is represented by these four musicians photographed in 2013. Alice Whitehouse (Tenor Horn), Emily Lounds (Tenor Horn), Rosie Keeling (Trombone.), and Jack Davies (Trumpet).

Chapter 5
Gornal at Work

Work in the Gornals has historically been associated with quarrying and mining, with brick-making and brick-laying, and at one time the cottage industry of nail-making. The clothes trade was represented by Clifford Williams, and there have also been a number of engineering firms associated with the district.

Some of these activities were covered in "Volume 1", and here is an opportunity to return to the world of work in the Gornals.

Right: Derek Greenaway and Fred Jones dig out the clay in a local pit near The Alley in 1950.
(Lee Photos)

Below: By way of contrast, the mineral products of the Gornal area were finally removed by a massive opencast site operated by Murphy Brothers in the 1970s and 80s. The site is seen here from Dibdale Road, looking across towards the Russells Hall Estate and Barrow Hill. (Paul Roberts)

97

Open-cast mining

Above: The huge open-cast site seen from the Himley Road side looking back towards the Burton Road Hospital building. (NW)
Left: One of Murphy's large tippers used on the site. In the background are houses in "The Graveyard". (Paul Roberts)

Bottom left: One of Murphy's lorries climbs Dibdale Lane on leaving the site. (Paul Roberts)

Murphy Brothers of Thurmaston, Leicestershire, worked this open-cast site from 1968 until 1971, turning over the earlier workings once exploited by Gibbons. It had a huge impact on the area and paved the way for eventual redevelopment of the area for housing.

Gibbons had been a major employer in the Gornals, in the company's pits, and the works on either side of Dibdale Lane. (See pages 50/51 of "Volume1".)

Right: As late as 1979 the Gibbons Group opened a new Technical Laboratory at the Dibdale Lane site to carry out research and testing of the company's refractory and building products. It was built on the site of a former warehouse which had been destroyed by fire. The £360.000 building covered 16,000 sq.ft. and was built with the group's own "Ravenhead" brown rusticated bricks. Dr. Ralph Heeley took charge of the new lab with John Eccles as his deputy, and Brian Troman as lab manager.

Centre right: A new "works office" also crept into the site but was to be short-lived. Ironically the building survives today as a snooker club.
(John Parker Collection)

Bottom right: Looking across part of the Gibbons site during demolition. On the skyline are three apartment blocks at Eve Hill, Dudley. Only one of these towers still stands today. Bottom left: The Mobious Strip of firebrick in the 1979 building.
(John Parker Collection)

GWB Furnaces

GWB Furnaces was another company that grew out of the Gibbons' activities in the vast area between Himley Road, Dibdale Lane and Jews Lane, not forgetting other Gibbons ventures in the Pensnett area!

GWB Furnaces was created as a private company in 1931 and made great progress in the production of boilers and furnaces and the associated engineering. The "public face" of the company was the fine office building built overlooking Jews Lane (see "Volume 1" page 31). However the real industrial activity went on in a less visible area behind that building, and now partly covered by an industrial estate.

Left: Cliff Edwards, a native of Club Row, became a refractory bricklayer and is seen here working at GWB Furnaces in the early 1950s. He was also known locally as an amateur boxer. He and his partner Alfie Walker took part in some of the first fights staged at the Baggeridge Miners' Social Club in the late 1940s.

Cliff is also to be found in the staff picture at the top of the page! (It includes all sections of the firm's workforce.) Cliff is wearing a cap and boiler suit and is near the centre of the photograph!
(Joan Webb)

Bricks

Brick-making and brick-laying were both activities that employed a lot of people in the Gornals. Looking at the 1911 census one finds house after house occupied by miners and brick-makers & brick layers.

Right; Sam Harris (1898-1984) was the son of Bill and Phoebe Harris – Bill being a bricklayer. Sam grew up in Moden Hill, Ruiton, and, like his father, became a bricklayer, after serving with the Gloucesters in the First World War. He married Rose Marsh of Gornal Wood and they went to live in Musk Lane and later Wood Road. He was sociable person and dedicated pigeon flier.

Above: This picture seems inspired by the famous picture of steel erectors at work in New York. Sam Harris is standing on the top right of the picture. His brother – Tom Harris – is fifth from the right. Standing on the left is William Harris – father of Tom and Sam. Front right is Albert Marsh – brother in law to Sam, or Rose's brother!. (Both pictures: Mary Jordan)

Men at Work

Left: Reg Price and Bert Hudson working at C.E. Marshall's works, now used as storeroom by Eggingtons, but seen in "Volume 1" as Abbey Tyres – page 62 . Mr. Marshall ran a small plating and engineering business in the centre of Gornal Wood until going on to greater things in Wolverhampton.

Reg Price was the son of Hiram and Louisa Price, and nephew to Hiram Price – the preacher! Reg had workd for Gibbons in a clay pit but later stayed at Marshalls until his retirement.
(Val Cartwright)

Below: Arnold Ball and Dick Blackham working at Arnold's cobbling business in Jews Lane in 1976. Arnold started the business about 1935, and was joined by Dick in 1946.
(Express & Star photo from the collection of Margaret Sargeant)

Bottom left: Bert Hughes with his coal lorry, delivering Baggeridge coal to customers in the Gornals. Bert, who grew up in a family from Tansey Green, lived at Five Ways. (Lily Porter)

Centre left: No one has yet produced pictures of Gornal's gas works at work but Graham Clark has found his father's ID card issued while working at the gas works!

Vanished industry...

Spread around the Gornals were a number of industrial enterprises that have now disappeared, in some places the sites are put to new use, at others all traces of the past are hidden by new housing.

Right: The Fibre-Form factory occupied a site just off The Holloway, and introduced "new industry" to the Gornals, in the form of the manufacture of fibre pressings – once used to form the backs of TV and radio sets, and in the motor industry.
(Keith Bayliss)

Centre Right: Tucked away behind Walter Mills garage and coach depot (See "Volume 1" pages 169-173) was "S & W Fireplaces", established in the 1930s as the "S & W Glazed Tile Company" by Walter Mills and Ron Geary. After the War the firm diversified into fitting gas fires and fireplaces.

Bottom Right: The Musk Lane trading estate on the site of the gas works, which closed at the end of the seventies.

Sedgley Urban District Council established its own gas-works down in Gornal Wood. The council took over an existing inefficient works and rebuilt it – opening the new plant on 29th October 1883. The gas holders became a familiar part of the local skyline! Two members of the Brettlell family managed the works, and a number of local people worked there.

Part of the gas works complex survives and provides a home to the Musk Lane Trading Estate as seen in this picture.

Deepdale Engineering

Left to right: David Nock, (Managing Director), Arthur Nock (one of the founders of the firm), Tim Coles (a sales director), John Marsh (company secretary), and Michael Beardsmore (President of Dudley & Sandwell Chamber of Commerce), celebrating fifty years of business in 1999.
(Sue Windmill)

Deepdale Engineering was started by Harry Cashmore and Arthur Nock in 1949, and first used modest premises in Deepdale Lane – hence the name. They employed many Gornal people. Harry Cashmore's daughter – Mary – married Julian Woodall (See the chapter on Scouting!.) Julian became an employee in the firm.

The firm later left its Gornal roots and became established in Peartree Lane and then Pedmore Road, Dudley, where it still exists today. While specialising in metal fabrication and pipe work, it has developed skills in what would be described as "heritage engineering". It has been able to contribute to preservation of a Sentinal Steam lorry, a replica Trevitihic locomotive of 1801, traction engine restoration, and produce parts for the Jubilee Trust's sailing ship, "Tenacious".

Centre left: Left to right: Harry Cashmore and Arthur Nock (directors), Jimmy Simpkiss, George Skidmore, Albert Cooke and Tom Cooke, all engineers, plau the driver from Males Transport. (Mary Woodall)

Bottom left: When you see Morris' Sentinal steam lorry on the road – think – this was made possible by a firm that began in The Gornals

Rounds Bakery at work.

The firm of H.A.D. Round set up in Prospect Row, Gornal Wood, when Tom Round and his son Des moved their bakery from King Street, Netherton, in 1945. Father and son doubled as bakers and delivery men, Des eventually taking over from his father. By 1973 the firm had forty four employees and four shops. The firm used the building once used by Ben Williams to produce hearth furniture (see "Volume 1" page 86).
As they said in Gornal, "Mr. Round is in charge of rounds and Mr. Baker is in charge of baking."

Right: Doreen Hall and Pearl Fellows, known as "The Swiss Roll Duo".

Bottom left: Chief Baker, Ray Baker, preparing some marzipan.

Bottom right: Des Round (in the background) is supervising the girls in the foreground who are in the packing department.

Round's Bakery: *Above: George Price, with a tray on his shoulder, retires from Rounds in 1980, having worked there for thirty years. Des Round (on the left) leads staff in saying farewell. (Jem Evans)*
Below left: Gwen Payton seen preparing pie cases. Below right: Bill Griffiths was one of the people who worked at Rounds all their working life. (John Smith Collection)

Delivering Fruit & Veg

At one time brick-laying, or mining, provided work from generation to generation. Today we find that delivering fruit and veg in the Gornals has passed through three generations of one family: the Hales.

The business was started by Isaac Hale Snr. who was a miner at Baggeridge Colliery, but he left the pit during the 1921 coal strike and started a fruit and veg round, using a small push cart.

Above: Isaac Hale Snr's two sons, Isaac Jnr. and Donald, carried on the fruit and veg business and are seen here on their round, using a proper cart and their horse, "Boxer". Donald's son Adrian is seen on the front of the cart.

Right: Donald Hale, born 1931, and his son Adrian, born 1967, are seen here with the mobile greengrocery van currently used by Adrian. Adrian had trained as an engineer but was eventually persuaded to become the third generation running the business.

(Pictures from the Hale Family Collection)

Delivering Fruit & Veg

Donald Hale's first van to become a mobile greengrocery shop was a converted mobile library. Donald passed his driving test in 1952, after returning home from National Service. Billy Timmins, wholesale fruit and veg man from Bird Street, gave him a tip-off that this van was available and the delivery of fruit & veg was modernised overnight.

Left: Donald and the first van out on deliveries.

Belwow: Donald Hale with the current mobile greengrocery shop, seen at work in Boundary Crescent in 2015. Adrian took over after Donald's forced retirement in 1992.

Left: Upper Gornal's best known fruit & veg man has to be Sammy Jeavons (See page 185). Here he is seen on his round in Dudley's Priory Estate in the sixties. Sammy retained the use of horse and cart longer than anyone else.
(Betty Caddick Collection)

Working at Baggeridge Colliery

In "Volume 1" some consideration was given to the extent that Baggeridge Colliery was the major employer and provider of work in the Gornals. Although the leaflet produced at the time of closure (right) suggested that the colliery had a life stretching from 1895 until 1968, it did not begin full production of coal until 1912. After the First World War, coal mining began a long decline in the other pits in the area and other kinds of work took over the working lives of local people. It is debatable how much the Baggeridge Pit did dominate the local labour scene. One informant recalling the 1930s of her childhood assured me that all the men she knew were miners (when describing the congregation at Lake Street Chapel), but during the colliery's final decade it had to bring in workers from a wide area. Once we have the chance to see the census returns for the decades after 1911, I think we will see evidence that mining underwent a long decline in importance to the Gornals, during the time that Baggeridge "struggled on".

Above: In this aerial photograph of the pit notice its isolation from urban life – it was not quite "on the doorstep" as in many mining communities. The shafts occupy the centre of the picture while the screens and wagon-loading facilities are to the right.
(Joanne Robinson collection)

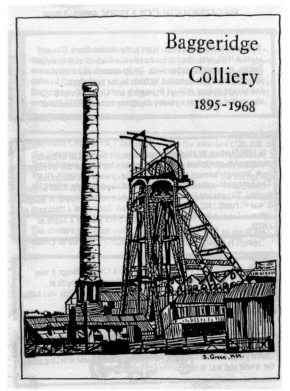

Baggeridge Colliery 1895-1968

Above: A sketch of the frame and landmark chimney at Baggeridge Colliery was used to decorate the front of a leaflet produced when the Baggeridge Country Park opened on the site of the pit.

Above – a lonely mine surveyor stands in one of the main underground "drives" of Baggeridge Colliery in a picture that captures the atmosphere of the pit. Vic Smallshire (1945 – 2014) was born in Wolverhampton. After an engineering course at Bilston College he obtained a job as a trainee mining surveyor at Baggeridge Colliery about 1961. He had a lifelong love of "holes in the ground" and became very interested in the life and times of the pit. When the pit closed in 1968 he worked in other pits for a year but then left the industry for another surveying career. His great contribution to the Black Country was the part he played in saving the Dudley Canal Tunnel. (Picture made available by Robert Smallshire)

Centre left: Two miners at Baggeridge Colliery work with a hydraulic pit prop in a photograph taken to show local people at work for a brochure prepared for a Methodist Conference in the early 60s. (BCS Collection)

Left: the Black Country Society, then in its infancy, produced this medallion to commemorate Baggeridge Collier, and to mark its closure. When the night shift workers emerged from the pit early in the morning of 2nd March 1968 they were met by four members of the Society; Dr. John Fletcher, John Brimble, M.Watson and H. Bowater. They presented medallion no.2 to Mr. B. Fellows of Lower Gornal – the longest serving member of the shift – and one of the few who lived locally! Two thousand of these medallions were produced at theend of 1967 and were sold for twenty-five shillings each (£1.25).

Above: In 1958 the winding gear at Baggeridge Colliery was changed from steam-powered to electrical power. These men worked continuously in two twelve hour shifts to complete the work during a shut-down period between 25th July and 10th August. (Both pictures: Joanne Robinson Collection)

Below: thirty years after the pits' closure, former miners gather at Baggeridge Country Park, in 1998 to witness the unveiling of a sheet metal statue made by Steve Field to commemorate the work of such men. The event was organised by South Staffordshire District Council.

Many men who had worked in the Earl of Dudley's earlier pits transferred to Baggeridge Colliery after 1912. In turn, their sons and grandsons worked at the pit – creating whole "dynasties" of mean associated with Baggeridge. A good example is the Darby family.

*Left: Walter Darby dressed a member of the Rescue Brigade Walter's father was William Henry Darby who left school in 1885 to work in a local pit, later transferring to Baggeridge where he worked thirty years. (Sixty three years altogether as a miner.) He was awarded the BEM in 1941 and the Earl of Dudley gave him £50 for services to mining. William married Charlotte at St. James' in 1883 and they had three sons. The second son was Walter, born in 1898. Walter followed his father down the pit, and progressed by taking every possible step to improve himself. In the end he served forty six years at Baggeridge. Walter married Florence on Christmas Day 1916 – also at St. James'. He was appointed Under Manager at Baggeridge on 1ˢᵗ November 1943. Walter's son's, Alfred (born 1928) and Joseph Darby (born 1920), also worked at the pit.. Alf, who was a carpenter, was at the pit when it closed.
(Helen Birch Collection)*

Below left: Edward Jones (1901-1985) worked all his life at Baggeridge Colliery, and is seen here with his wife Sarah after receiving a BEM for services to mining. He, like Walter Darby, progressed at the pit and became captain of a rescue team. (With his experience of working with explosives he was made a leiutenant in the Home Guard, although like other miners, he refused to drill!) In the pit rose to the rank of Deputy, then Overman. He was active member of Lake Street Methodist Chapel – where Sarah's father had been a founder trustee. (Muriel Brown collection)

Below right: In "Volume 1" we were able to identify a Baggeridge miner with pit pony as Don Morris (see page 179). Here is another picture of Don with one of the pit's ponies.
(Sue Windmill)

112

Chapter 6
Sporting Gornal

The Gornals seemed to have spawned a large number of sports teams, some of which were described in Chapter 7 of "The Gornals" on "Events and Organisations. Sports teams were attached to the schools, to the chapels, pubs and to larger employers, and it seems that many people from the Gornals "graduated" through these, and on into other professional and amateur sporting organisations, stretching far outside the Gornals.

Right: Many young Gornalites had their first experience of playing in a sports team while at school. For example: here see the Robert Street School Footballers. Here is the 1953/4 side which became runners-up in the local school league against Park Lane, Tipton. Back row: Joe Cooper, Joe Marsh, Julian Woodall, Roy Southall, Graham Clarke, Joe Bradley, Bob Simmons, Alan Cornfield. Front row: Billy Watton, Billy Timmins, Harold Hickman, Roy Beards (captain), Melvin Wilkinson, Bob Geary and John Bunn. The teacher in both pictures is Mr. Phipps. (Alan Cornfield later signed professional forms for Shrewsbury FC.)

Right: The Robert Street S.M. Team of 1950: Back: Roy Guest, John Collins, Frank Whitehouse, Alan Hudson, Frank Marsh, Billy Weswtood, John Allen. Front: Ivor Bradley, George Allen, Len Cooper (Captain – later signed for Wolves), Harold Westwood & Bert Harris. (Graham Clarke)

The Gibbons Sports Club.

The sports teams associated with the Gibbons company were mentioned in the pages devoted to "Industrial Lower Gornal" in Volume 1 (pages 51, 52). The success of the Gibbons sports teams must have very much the result of the company's support and provision of proper facilities.

Before the Second World War there had been discussion at Gibbons' Dibdale Works about developing ground opposite the company's canteen. In the first instance this would have been a "garden of rest" to be used by past and present employees. After the war, this concept expanded to become the provision of a proper sports club on the Dibdale site.

These new playing fields were created at the same time as the firm levelled an area north of Dibdale Lane for a new tunnel-kiln. They greatly extended the scope of sporting activities associated with the firm, although there had long been a great tradition of the firm having a successful cricket team.

The club was to be opened on 29th April 1950 with great ceremony. President of the Sports Club was Lt. Colonel William Gibbons, his brother Eric being named as one of several "vice presidents".

William's wife should have performed the opening ceremony at 2.30pm on that date, followed a quarter of an hour later by Mrs. D. E. Little opening the tennis court. This was none other than Dudley's famous tennis player, Dorothy Round.

The first bowling match to be played that afternoon on the new bowling green was between the Gibbons team, captained by S. Brownhill, and the team from the Gornal Miners Welfare Club. The first cricket match was to be played against the Dudley Cricket Club team. The Gibbons team was captained by S. Cartwright and included messrs. Clarke, Crawford, Davies, Hart, Hodgetts, Kendall, Watson, Wrightson and York.

Unfortunately the event was ruined by heavy rain and the opening had to be postponed until 4 o' clock, and only two hundred people turned out to see Mrs. Gibbons perform a short ceremony at the gates. The bowls and cricket matches had to be

Below: The Gibbons Cricket Team of 1967, when they won the League Championship (Division 1) of the Wolverhampton & District League. (They were runners up in 1970 and again in 1971).
Back row: Gerald Jones, John Smith, Don Yorke, Ralph Oakley, Ralph Jordan, Cedric Fellows and Tom Willis (Umpire). Front Row: Graham Clarke, Ken Fradgley, Arthur Timmins, John Lampitt, and Ian Cole.
(Graham Clarke Collection)

postponed and Dorothy Little promised to return another day to give some free tennis lessons! Despite the weather a line up for a press photograph was assembled, featuring W. Hart (Club Secretary), Mr. J. Allen (company chief cashier and club treasurer), Mr. W. Cooksey (Bowling Green superintendent) and Mrs. Gibbons.

The work, which had already taken three years, was not completed. The clubhouse had to be erected after the opening and included facilities for billiards, snooker, table tennis, and darts, and was provided with a bar. These activities complemented the outside provision for cricket, football, tennis, bowls, croquet, hockey and netball.

Right: Gibbons Cricket Club team photographed on their home-ground in Dibdale Road in 1970. Note the pavilion in the back ground. Left to right: back row: Horace Holding, John Smith, Glyn Hale, John Lampitt, Arthur Timmins.
Front row: Derek Bell, Terry Brooke, Graham Clarke, Terry Jones, Ralph Oakley and A. Smelding.
(Graham Clarke collection)

Right: An early Gibbons Football team line outside their "pavilion". Back row: Jack Rock, Ray Simmons, ?, ?, Wilf Crawford, Horace Ball, David Knowles, ?
Front row: ?,?, Joe Banks, ?,?,?.
(Marion Savory collection)

Top Left: An awards evening at the Gibbons Sports Club.
Cricket Awards: Back row: Bill Hyde, David Knowles, Wilf Crawford, James Alexander,? Jimmy Wrightson, Horace Ball. Front row: ?, Arthur Timmins, Jack Clarke , J. Wrigtson, (and Steve Williams?)
(Marion Savory Collection)

Centre Left: A damaged picture of a Gibbons cricket team, reproduced here to illustrate the way that the Burton Road Hospital formed a background to the Gibbons sports ground.
(Margaret Sargeant)

Below: Tennis players from the Gibbons Sports Club. ?, Walter Wickstead, ?.?.?.?. Bill Passmont Front row: Marion Savory, Thelma Hemmings, Frankie Lane, ?, Margaret Sargeant and Marion ?. Margaret won that year's Tennis Cup.
(Margaret Sargeant)

The "Evening Institutes" held at Red Hall School and Robert Street were homes to football teams. The team at Red Hall is featured in Volume 1, pages161 & 194).These provided teams in which local lads who had left school could continue to play football.

This is the 1956 team from Robert Street. Left to right, back row: J. Woodhall, R. Southall, J.Moss, W.Brownhill, Brian Hunt.. Front Row: J. Marsh, G. Smith. R. Harris, J. Fellows and Arthur Hunt. (Jim Fellows Collection)

Arthur Hunt

Arthur Hunt was representing Robert Street Institute in the sem- final of the West Bromwich Shield in 1958 when he collided with the other team's goalkeeper. Despite continuing to take part in the game, he was later admitted to hospital and it was found that he had damaged his pancreatic tube. He died fourteen weeks later – two weeks before he was due to be married. A memorial game was held on 15th November 1958 at the Garden Walk Stadium. The match was between the Tipton, Coseley & Sedgley Youth Team led by Brian Hunt, and "Colwyn Bay" –a team made up of TV actors from the "Army Game" including Ted Lune. (Alfie Bass and Bill Fraser were unable to play.) The match was won by the local side: 3-2, before a large crowd, and prizes were presented by Bert Williams (the Wolves and England player).

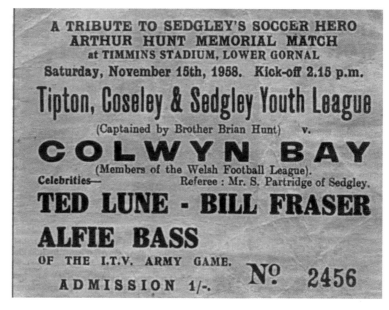

Right: Brian Hunt, Arthur's brother, with members of the Hunt Family plus Arthur's fiancée at the Memorial Match. Ted Lune in cloth cap.
The following year the Arthur Hunt Memorial Trophy was launched.

Left: The Red Hall Institute's football team of 1949, in the school's playground overlooked by the back of the Alexandra Cinema. Back row: Bernard Beardsmore, Harold Langford, Fred Abbiss, Eric Potts, Bill Ball and Mick Dunn (Trainer). Front row: Ron Oakley, Alan Meredith, J.R. Baker, Harold Raybould, Derek Jones, Derek Hughes and Barry Lloyd.
(Harold Raybould Collection)

Left: In October 1998 a reunion was held at the British Legion for lads who had played in the Red Hall Institute's football teams. Left to right, back row: Ron Flavell, Melvin Wilkinson, Trevor Smith, Michael Lock, Trevor Smallman, Derrick Walker, Stan Greenaway, Graham Clarke, Michael Harvey. Jerry Lloyd. Front row: Des Foster, Billy Nock, Sid Middleton, Fred Middleton.
(Graham Clarke – who also supplied a picture of the club's badge.)

Bottom left: Red Halll Evening Institute/Youth Club footballers of the sixties. Second from the right on the front row is Melvin Morson who appears in several other pictures.
(Diane and Terry Kinsella)

Upper Gornal Rangers

Also known as "Bridgewood's Eleven", because the team was led by youth club leader Bill Bridgewood. Back row: John Harris, Ken Jeavons, Les Fellows, Graham Clarke, Ray Slater, John Cotton, John Bird, and Bert Pearson (Trainer). Front row: George Hollis, Mervyn Travis, Brian Westwood, Derek Edwards, Cliff Fellows and Don Jones. Five of these players signed for other local Football League clubs, but John Harris, the captain, signed for the Wolves and later played for Walsall. Here they pose with the Wood Shield, won in 1956/7. The building in the background survives on the "rec" at Upper Gornal and is currently a gym. (Graham Clarke)

Centre right: The Upper Gornal Rangers of 1957/58 when they reached the finals in the Wood Shield and the W.B.A. Shield. Back row: Bill Bridgewood, Tony Steventon, George Burns, Graham Clarke, David Young, Graham Bradley, and Bert Pearson (Trainer). Front row: Ivan Andrews, Melvin Trevis, Melvin Wilkinson, John Cotton (captain), Frank Millard, Jeff Attwood and Bruce Hovington. (Melvin Wilkinson)

Bottom right: Melvin Wilkinson and Melvin Travis display the Wood Shield and W.B.A. Shield Melvin had been a "Marley Champion" – a great Marbles player – had collected over a thousand marbles and played regularly on the "pitch" in front of The White Chimneys... When he left school he worked in the Drawing Office at GWB.
Bottom left: Bert Pearson and Bill Bridgewood, both of whom worked hard to nurture the Rangers.

Lower Gornal Athletic Club Football Team

Above: The Peacocks in 1965/66. Left to right: back row: Mick Babb, Alan Johnson, Brian Hunt (temporary goal keeper), Alan Hawkes, Paddy Page. Front row: Alan Cornfield, Maurice Hackett, Gordon Smith (Captain), George Andrews, Barry Samsome and Alan Fullwood. (Gordon Smith Collection)

The football team that inhabits the Garden Walk Stadium in Lower Gornal has a history stretching back to the early years after the First World War when it adopted the name Lower Gornal Athletic to distinguish itself from other teams. The team was based at The Fiddlers Arms and played on a ground in Brick Kiln Lane. It was led by Isaac Bradley.

A revived version of the club moved into the Garden Walk Stadium after the Second World War when old pit banks were levelled and drained and a football ground created by local enthusiasts. (See page 89 of "Volume 1".) At first it was eventually called the John Timmins Stadium after one of its leading benefactors.

The club joined the Worcestershire Combination League in 1951 and then the West Midlands League in 1962. This was followed by one of the periods of the club's success – success itself tending to come in waves. Fred Whittall joined the club as manager and recruited semi-professional players – paid for by a very successful lottery run by the club. Money could also be raised by transfers and two players earned a record transfer fee for the club when George Andrews and Gary Bell went to Cardiff City for £2100 in 1965. George Andrews later returned to the Black Country to play for Walsall.

During this 1960s "heyday" the players still had to train on the ash car park next to the ground – lit by car headlights – on Tuesday and Thursday nights.

The Peacocks (Lower Gornal Athletic Club football team) through the ages:

Lower Gornal Athletic FC, 1919/20 Back row: players: Harry Timmins, ? and Joe Cooper. Middle row: Les Hickman, D. Wakelam, and Percy Beardsmore. Front row: Len Cooper, Job Jones, W, Woodhall (Captain), Jack Jones and Alf Jones. The man seated in the left foreground is Mr. Jones Snr., father of the other three Jones and known as "Billy 'on the hob' Jones". Len Cooper, who became a professional footballer, was the son of Len Cooper Snr., famous cobbler of Summit Place.
(Julie Pitt)

Lower Gornal Athletic Club FC in 1948. Taken near The Bulls Head.
(Margaret Sargeant)

Below: The Peacocks in 2015.

Sports Teams at Pubs

Another way of pursuing sporting interests was joining local pub teams.

Above: Footballers from the White Chimneys. Left tor right: back row: A. Witton (Manager), T.Nicklin, J. Bannister, M.Spence, A. Dudley, G. Jones, G.Smith, G. Hill, T. Newell (trainer). Front row: M.Rose, T. Price, W. Smith, C. Spence, M. Hill, M. Edwards. The team played in the Division Three of the Dudley League. (Julie Pitt Collection)

Centre left: Footballers from the Bulls Head in the 1970s. Only Maurice Bache, second from left on the front row, and John Andrews, far right on the front row, have been identified in this picture. (Julie Pitt Collection)

Bottom left: Footballers from The Bush, about 1974. David Griffiths, John Smith, Ronny Horton, Stan Witton, Mickey Stevens, Peter Dobson, Keith Bayliss, Steve Greenaway, Richard Smallman, Patrick Collins, & Ian Hollis. (Keith Bayliss Collection)

Individual sportsmen

As well as local teams there are numerous Gornal sportsmen who have joined teams elsewhere and sportsmen who have taken part in individual sports.

*Right: **Gordon Bentley** was born in 1938 in Hurst Hill. His connection with The Gornals was established when he saw a derelict cottage on the Himley Road, next to the chapel, and decided it would make an ideal home – it was derelict and had no electricity connections, and was flooded but there were "roses round the door". He was later attracted to a similar property in Chase Road.*

Gordon's great talent was long-distance running and he joined Tipton Harriers in 1952, both he, and his brother Ron, became leading runners in the club. He achieved various world records and won many trophies and ran for his country in the Comrades Marathon – a sixty mile run – in South Africa, won by the Harriers in 1972.

His training included running to and from work and in the many open spaces surrounding the Gornals. Further connection with Gornal was made when he and his wife Liz opened a Sports-wear shop in Louise Street, although this was a venture that only lasted about three years.

Gordon and Liz also joined the Bowling Club attached to the Baggeridge Miners Social Club and Liz can still be found as an active member of that club today. Gordon died in December 2003 at the age of 65.

Indoor Sports

Snooker, Darts, and Dominoes have been popular indoor "sports" in the Gornals.
Below: Jim Watton (centre) and team-mates are seen here collecting snooker trophies.

Playing bowls has been a popular sporting activity in the Gornals. The Silver Oaks Bowling Club was established at the Memorial Hall in September 2005, led by Mary Woodall and Mary Timmins. It originally set out to raise funds for repairs to the church bell tower, but has been meeting regularly on Thursday afternoons ever since. Left to right: back row: Norma Cartwright, Jean Edwards, Bill Sutton, Gordon Cook, Stan Portman, Rita Harrison, Catherine Harrison, Ron Finch. Seated: Chris Walsh, Joyce Bridgewater, Joy Price, Olive Napier, Hilda Marsh, Mary Finch, Front: Mary Timmins, Tim Woodall, and Mary Woodall. Below: The Baggeridge Miners Social Club bowling team meets on the green established alongside the Baggeridge Miners Social Club. Although the club (seen in the background) opened in 1941, the grounds around it were not opened until 31st March 1951 when I.W. Cumberbatch, Chairman of the NCB, came along to perform the ceremony.

Chapter 7
Pubs and Clubs

Looking at photographs of Gornal's past one can see very clearly that a great deal of the social life of the community once took place in pubs and clubs. This received some coverage in "Volume 1" and we return to the topic here.

As well as the pubs with their sporting activities, there are the clubs with political affiliations, and specialist interests. Both Upper Gornal and Gornal Wood have special designated buildings to provide a home for pensioners' clubs, and in Lower Gornal we have the British Legion club just off Ruiton Street. Of course, some pubs have disappeared, and there now seems to be no sign of the Friendly Societies. Some pubs and clubs seem to leave very few records of their existence so maybe there is lots more to discover and explore in this area of the past.

Many pubs held annual "Harvest Festivals" where produce was auctioned for charity.

Top Right: Billy Wright, the Wolves and England footballer, came to Gornal to open a Harvest Festival at The Red Lion. David Haden is in the centre of the picture with his brother, Derek, on the right. Almost hidden is Martin Roper, and at the back is David Oakley. On the left is Michael Grainger – son of Fred Grainger who ran a grocery shop on Himley Road. (Derek Haden Collection)

Bottom Right: Sammy Jeavons at a "Harvest Produce" auction at the Dudley Lodge of the Royal Antediluvian Order of Buffalos in 1963. He is being assisted by his daughter Betty, seen on the left of the picture – who supplied the picture.

Pubs

Drinkers at The Pear Tree:

Many of Gornal's "characters" met at the pubs. Second from the right is "Jackory" – seen leading a Coronation parade in "Volume 1" – page 4.
On the right is Wilf Haden, in the middle is Arthur Evans, on the left are Billy Harmon and Mr. Edwards.
(Derek Haden Collection)

Centre left: An excellent view of The Pear Tree, Gornal Wood, – one of the area's lost pubs. At the time the licensee was Matilda Jones, who was the widow of Isaac Jones who had been licensee until his death in 1904.
(John Parker Collection)

Below: Ladies at The Fiddler's Arms. This pub has played a part in many activities in Gornal Wood – providing a home for Methodists, Scouts and pigeon – flyers... Suddenly in 2015 it appeared on a list of pubs that might be turned into Co-op stores!
(Dave Evans)

The Cross Keys
Top right: A children's room at The Cross Keys, Ruiton Street, Lower Gornal, was known as "The Clinic", and was used as a place for up to twenty women to meet on most nights! From the left; Mrs. Parker, Kathy Smith, who ran The Cross Keys, Madeleine Prosser and her Mum, Eileen Martin and Frances Watkins. The Cross Keys survives as a building but is no longer a pub.
(Julie Pitt Collection)

The Jolly Crispin
Centre right: Serious activity for men down at the local: men of the darts team at The Jolly Crispin, Upper Gornal.
Colin Edwards, ?, Alfie Walker, ?,?, Roy Webb and Cliff Edwards Jnr.
The Cross Keys continues to be a successful pub in Upper Gornal and runs its own annual beer festival.
(Collection of Joan Webb)

The Durham Ox
Bottom Right: Party Time at The Durham Ox, Hill Street, Ruiton: every Easter the men had to lift the women up and the next day the roles were reversed. In 1974 Mrs. Mary Griffiths, the landlord's wife, attempts to lift Don Smart, while Stan Greenaway loses his grip on Mrs. Fanny Hale.
The Durham Ox survives as a building but is no longer a pub.
(Joanne Robinson Collection)

Losing pubs...

Top left: The Bricklayers Arms in Kent Street, Upper Gornal – pictured in "Volume 1", page 14, as "The Pig on the Wall". Known to everyone as "Hammonds" it was boarded-up and awaiting its fate when this picture was taken.
(John Parker

Centre left: The Crown at the top of Holloway Street, Ruiton, seen from the graveyard of the Ruiton Chapel. (See page 29 of "Volume 1")
The building is now the headquarters of a swimming pool supplier.
(John Parker)

Below: The Good Intent in Vale Street, Ruiton. The pub is currently closed and boarded up.
(Vilma Carter)

Above: The Cottage of Content, in Clarence Street, Upper Gornal, became known as "The Cabin" and for many years was run successfully by Jim Riley. The regulars, seen above, in 1973, are seated around the trophies won for darts, dominoes, and football. The pub survives as a building but is now an Italian restaurant. (Betty Caddick's Collection)

Right: The Cork Club at the Bulls Head, Himley Road, Gornal Wood. The club met every Sunday and raised money for charity. Jim Wright collects "fines" from members who have failed to observe the dress code. The club was launched by the landlord, Sid Hale.
(Joanne Robinson Collection)

Regulars at The Limerick, Summit Place, Gornal Wood. The Flavell family were regular users of this pub for several generations. Here, beginning fourth from left are Joe, Annie, Cousin Joe, Dan and Bill Flavell. The pub closed in 1999 and has been demolished.
(Joanne Robinson Collection)

The Crooked House

The Crooked House (The Glynne Arms) was a popular destination on Sunday afternoon for many Gornal folk, and photographs were sometimes taken in its environs. Back row, left; Rueben Kelly then unknown, then Olwyn Hale Tom Flavell ("Oakey"), Joby Bradley, and Fred Elegton. Front row: second from right: Joe Flavell, brother of Tom.
(Joanne Robinson Collection)

Refreshment Room,
Crooked House, Himley.

A selection of postcards were produced showing the wonders of The Crooked House, and these two come from the collection of George Harrison – the last man to show a film at "The Bump". Note that it says "The Crooked House, Himley" – the pub was just beyond the Gornal (Sedgley UDC) boundary.

THE CROOKED HOUSE, HIMLEY. NEAR WOLVERHAMPTON.

COPYRIGHT. G.E.L.

The British Legion's branch in Lower Gornal

Right: William Burrows photographed the opening of the British Legions new wooden headquarters by The Five Ways in 1948.

The Upper Gornal conservative Club

Below: The committee of the Upper Gornal Conservative Club about 1969/70.
Back row: Colin Danbury, Jess Smith, Bert Paskin, Derek Naylor, Joe Dudley, Harry Clark, Sam Jeavons, and Terry Bradley (Treasurer). Front row: Sim Jeavons, Walter Webb, David Stanley (President), and Horace Bowater (Secretary).

The British Legion in The Gornals seems to have started at The Wooodman, but after a couple of meetings moved to the room above the Co-op in Zoar Street. For a time Billy Buxton was secretary, and was responsible for organising dances, whist drives and harvest festivals. Herbert Oakley was one of the founder members, along with Bill Smit, Richard Hyde and Ernie Greenaway. From the Co-op room the Legion moved to premises in Temple Street and then to the hut built just off Ruiton Street, close to Five Ways. (John Timmins may have helped acquire the ground.) The present building opened in 1966.

Friendly Societies seem to have completely disappeared from the Gornals, however there were once lodges of the RAOB – "the Buffs" – at both Upper and Lower Gornal.

Here we see William Jones in his RAOB regalia, photographed on 3rd December 1953 when he received his Roll of Honour for attaining the order's highest degree.

William Jones joined The Buffs on 14th September 1928 and was made a "Knight of the Order of Merit" in May 1936. The lodge met at the Old Bulls Head, Himley Road, every Tuesday evening. At post-war meetings William played the drums while Fred Turner played the piano. One Buff song that seemed particularly popular was "Wheel 'Em In". Other buffs included Jim Bradley, Alf Bradley (well known chorister at St. James'), and Edwin Greenaway – and some meetings seem to have been attended by Dr. Cunningham. Years later he asked a patient to sing the song!

In later life William Jones joined the British Legion, suggesting that might have been something that other Buffs did when the lodges closed. William died in 1976 at the age of 77. Bel0w: His "Roll of Honour" and medal.
(Sheila Millard)

The Miners' Social Club

The club was opened in 1924 in the building that is now known as Kiedel House, Church Street. See picture, top right.) The club moved to new premises in Lake Street in 1969 but that building has now disappeared.

The secretary for thirty years was John Hickman, seen third from the left on the picture on the right. (Picture: Val Haywood)

(Previous secretaries had been J.L. Smith and Reuben Bate.)

Billy Butler (seen above) was often to be found at the club – a popular local comedian, and Entertainment Secretary of the club.)

The club put on film shows, wrestling, and variety entertainment on Friday night and weekends. The club also ran many great day-trips and organised Christmas parties for members' children.

Bottom right: The Upper Gornal Pensioners Club building in Clarence Street today – see next page for the history of this building and the club. (NW)

The Upper Gornal Pensioners Club

After the Second World War it was felt that a meeting place should be provided for the senior citizens of Upper Gornal. A meeting was held in the Guild Hall behind the Dudley Co-operative Society branch in Clarence Street on 6th March 1952 and a constitution was adopted for an Upper Gornal Pensioners Club. In the Chair was Councillor Jabez Felllows, the Secretary was H. Hunt and the treasurer was Mrs. A.M. Henderson. The aim of the group was described as "To provide facilities for education and recreation for the benefit of elderly people who lived in Upper Gornal." Being "elderly" was defined as being over sixty.

It is interesting to wonder if further meetings were held in the Co-op Guild Hall because it took some time for the proposed facilities to materialise. It could be that Sedgley Urban District Council provided the site and helped find a builder, but the club itself had to embark on fund-raising with collecting boxes in local pubs etc The site found was near the corner of Clarence Street and Highgate Street, and construction began in July 1957. The builders were Mulville Builders Ltd., of Wolverhampton. No architect has been identified. The hall and "facilities" were built at a cost of £2750.

The grand opening took place on Saturday 14th June 1958 and the opening itself was conducted by John Moss – the Chairman of the National Old Peoples Welfare Council – reflecting that provision of such facilities was a nationwide phenomenum. Councillor Fellows was still in the chair of the club and W.M. Jones had had some part in supervising construction – he was the SUDC Engineer. £600 had been contributed by The King George V Fund but apart from that finance had been provided by the members. (Even so the club was still short of £500 to complete payment for the hall!)

It was stated that the hall would be open six days a week and that whist drives and concerts would provide a large part of its activities. Currently it opens to the elderly on two afternoons a week.

In 1962 the trustees had to reorganise as a charity and Mrs. Ellen Dews became its administrator, her husband being Stan Dews, the SUDC councillor. Ann Bate and Jenny Shakespeare are also names associated with running the club. Today it is run by Betty Williams, assisted by Pat Thompson, and until recently by the late Margaret Peters. The building continues to be owned by the charitable trust and has become quite a local landmark.

Below: The U.G. Pensioners Club in 2015.

The Lower Gornal Darby & Joan Club.

The club was opened on 18th May 1957 (not the date stated on page 66 of "Volume 1"). *The opening party are seen above outside the new club building.*
Left to right: back row: Clr. Albert Oakley, Clr. G. Beswick, S. Marsh, Joe Timmins, and A. Bradley. Third row; Mrs. Darrick, Mrs. Hammond, Mrs. Jevons, Ernie Bradley, J. Thompson, Arthur Worton (Robert Street headmaster).
Second row: Mrs. Cox, Mrs. P. Hale, John Timmins, and A Jevons. Front row: Mrs. P. Hale, Mrs. D. Whitehouse, Mr. J. Gilbert. Miss Kathryn Gibbons, Bert Box, ? and Mr. C. Rollinson. Mr. Gilbert (veteran member) and Kathryn Gibbons (of the local firm) had performed the opening ceremony.
A great deal of fundraising had been undertaken by a domino league established at the Horse & Jockey in Deepdale Lane.
(Verna Spittle)

Above: The Lower Gornal Darby & Joan Club still opens for a pensioners' lunchtime session every Wednesday morning.
Left to right: Nellie Davies, Iris Russell, Verna Spittle, Sid Chambers, Joan Chambers, Vera Marsh, and Barbara Westwood. The club is now organised by Verna Spittle

The Baggeridge Miners Welfare Club

As can be seen from the programme on the right, this building was opened by the Earl of Dudley on 10th May 1941. However, the surrounding grounds were not fully opened until ten years later!

The premises include two bars, a snooker room and a large upstairs assembly room with stage.

One of the regular activities to be found at the club is the "Active Retirement" group regularly meeting on Tuesday mornings, led by the author of this book. The group began life in 1997, led by Marjorie Gaul.

Below: Members of the "Active Retirement", photographed during a "motorway stop" while on a trip during 2015. (NW)

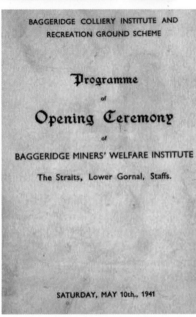

BAGGERIDGE COLLIERY INSTITUTE AND
RECREATION GROUND SCHEME

Programme
of
Opening Ceremony
of
BAGGERIDGE MINERS' WELFARE INSTITUTE

The Straits, Lower Gornal, Staffs.

SATURDAY, MAY 10th., 1941

Programme

5 p.m.   General Assembly outside main Entrance. J. Dando, Esq.,
Agent of the Earl of Dudley's Baggeridge Colliery
Limited will introduce the Rt. Hon. The Earl of Dudley, M.C., and
H. Atkinson, Esq., late District Organiser of the Miners' Welfare
Commission.

G. Warner, Esq., respresenting Messrs. Warner & Dean, the
Architects will present a Key to Mr. H. Atkinson.

Short speech by Mr. H. Atkinson, after which he will hand the
Key to the Earl of Dudley; he will also hand the Trust Deeds
to Mr. Lawson Price, Secretary to the Committee.

The Rt. Hon. The Earl of Dudley, M.C., will then insert the
Key into the lock, open the door and proceed into the Institute.

Members of the general public will follow into the Concert Hall
where they are requested to be seated.

Address by the Rt. Hon. The Earl of Dudley, M.C.

J. Jones, Esq., Secretary of the South Staffordshire and East
Worcestershire Miners' Association will propose a Vote of Thanks
to the Rt. Hon. The Earl of Dudley, M.C., which will be seconded
by B. Jefferies, Esq., District Organiser to the Miners' Welfare
Commission.

Mr. J. Dando will conclude the opening Ceremony.

7 p.m. A Concert will take place in the Concert Hall, for
programme see back page.

The Townswomen's Guild

We know from surviving 1930s church magazines that women's groups like the Mothers' Union and Ladies' Fellowships have long existed in The Gornals. Co-op history also tells us that there was a branch of the Co-operative Women's Guild meeting in Upper Gornal's Guild Hall before the Second World War. Unfortunately the records of such groups seem to become lost. Information regarding this Guild described here was sent form California!

The Gornal & District Branch of the Townswomen's Guild was started in the 1960s and met at the Baggeridge Miners' Club and later in St. Andrew's church hall, in The Straits. The first secretary was Mrs. J. Woodhall, and the first chairperson was Mrs. P.Hall. The group mounted quite ambitious concerts featuring their own choir, as well as all the usual Guild activities.

Above: Ladies of the Gornal & District Townswomen's Guild are seen here on an outing to Josiah Wedgewood's pottery at Barlaston about 1965. Third from the left on the front row is Vera Patrick who was chairperson of the branch. Later a Young Wives group was started at St. Andrew's – not to be confused with the TWG group!

Below: Left to right: Winnie Ward, Joan Price and Mary Lawton – all stalwarts of the Gornal Townswomen's Guild. (Pictures supplied by Jillian Dubois – all the way from California. Jillian is Joan Price's daughter.)

Above: The first meeting of the newly - formed Gornal Wood (Morning) Townswomen's Guild met on 16th September 2015 at the Darby & Joan Club in Abbey Street. Ann Wilson is the new secretary, Janet Spencer is in the Chair, and the treasurer is Joanne Robinson. (Joanne Robinson)

Below: The new TWG Committee, taking office in autumn 2015.
Left to right: Amanda Windmill, Janet Spencer, Margaret Sargeant, Ann Wilson, Jill Turley, Doreen Wedge, Sue Windmill, and Jayne Haywood (seated). (Joanne Robinson)

Chapter 8
Brewing, Keeping Pigs, and Flying Pigeons

A popular image of life in The Gornals in the past includes widespread home-brewing. Many folks did this to produce beer for their own consumption but some produced commercially on a small scale and were licensed to do so.

Let's take one home-brewer as a "case study". Ben Witton grew up in an old stone cottage in Stickley Lane, just off the Holloway. But in later life he lived in Red Hall Road opposite the chip shop – first run by the Brookses and then by the Bradleys. Ben worked at the Sunbeam in Wolverhampton and later as a shift manager at Round Oak Steel Works.

His real passion was home brewing and he usually produced about nine gallons every three weeks. At Christmas time he would produce up to thirty six gallons.

He bought his hops from Holdens and had to get up at four in the morning to "mash up" – fitting this in with his shift work.

When not brewing his own beer, the Gornalite, is often portrayed as rearing his own pig (or two), feeding his fowl, caring for his dog or looking after his pigeons! When local artist, Colin Hale, came to paint a definitive picture of Sammy Jeavons he was careful to include Sammy's chickens, although Sammy will always be remembered for his horses. What all this boils down to is that when folks from the countryside migrated into the Black Country, they brought elements of their rural life-style with them.

Photographs of all these aspects of local life have been difficult to find and therefore the chapter focuses on pigeon flying, before returning to the eternal Gornal subject of pigs and that particular "pig on the wall."

Above: Sally Williams, nee Perry, brewing at the Britannia pub in Upper Gornal in the 1940s. The pub had been in the Perry Family from 1874 until Sally's death in 1991. Six years after her death, the pub was acquired by Bathams, who still maintain a "Sally's room" in the pub today. As made clear in "Volume 1", this was just one of several Gornal area pubs where a butchery was also in operation on the premises. In the 1911 census the proprietor- Louis Peacock Perry – clearly statess his profession as butcher, although obviously licensee of the pub. Pictures of home-brewing are rare, so we have to be grateful for this image of commercial brewing. (Peter Glews Collection)

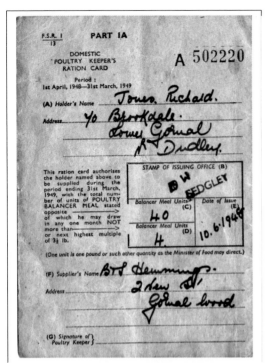

Left: A poultry-keeper's ration card from 1948 stating how much poultry meal he is entitled to, and identifying the local supplier. Obviously during the Second World War food rationing extended to one's livestock, but it is obvious from this card that such controls continued into the post-war era.
(Joanne Robinson Collection)

Centre left: George Jones' pigeon loft in Stickley Lane . George (1922-2000) worked at Baggeridge Pit, where he trained ponies, from leaving school until the pit closed. (He then worked at Allen's.) He was a flat-capped Woodbine smoking kind of guy who loved his family, his pigeons and his whippets. (Julie Pitt)

Centre right: Don Morris, and his dog "Whisky" take rest in front of the pigeon loft built at the family's home at 52 Cinder Road. This was bigger than the loft built at the previous family home and needed planning permission.
(Sue Windmill)

Julie and Sue give accounts of pigeon fliers on the next few pages.

Left: Ben Evans, proprietor of the Cosy Corner Café, with his pigeons, outside the loft at the back of 12 Abbey Road.
(Jem Evans)

Right: John Jones and his pigeon-flying trophies, about forty years ago.

Below: John Jones still caring for his pigeons in 2015, seen here in his traditional 10ft. loft. Despite having to work at a steel stock-holder's in Tipton seven days a week for thirty six years, John managed to look after the birds seven days a week as well – with help from his brother, William. He is the oldest member still racing at the Flying club based at The Fiddler's Arms.

"Dad's pigeons"
By Sue Windmill

When my sister and I were young we used to help Dad with his pigeons – as we had no brother who could do the job. Dad used to say that pigeons are a "365-day job", and that if you had animals you had to look after them right. No wonder Mum said when she married Dad, "All he came with was a pen-full of pigeons and a dog."

When the young were born I loved to hold them – so warm, but so funny-looking. I recall that Dad used to pair the pigeons on Valentines Day. As they grew up Dad would train them to come home. My sister and I would walk with the basket to the bottom of Barrow Hill for the first "loose", and then we would go a bit farther every week. Someone with a van would eventually take them to the common, and then to Hartlebury – it would cost Dad about 3p a bird. Sometimes they would take them to Brierley Hill station and they would take a longer journey by rail.

Friday night was pigeon night and we would take the pigeons to The Woodman Inn – the club from which Dad flew the birds. The club was named "Gornal Wood West End Flying Club". The birds were booked in and had a rubber ring put on their leg. Dad would pool his best birds, like betting on

horses but for smaller stakes. We would then bring the clock back with us – ready for Saturday. Sometimes the birds would go on a Thursday if they had to go "over the water" to France.

Everything would be ready for the arrival of the birds. The pen was cleared, and the clock would be ready on the front of the pen. My sister and I would make journeys up to The Woodman to see if the birds had been "tossed". In the window would be a small board stating what time this had happened and details of the wind. We would then have to run and tell Dad.

When the birds arrived the rubber band had to be taken off and it was put in a small capsule, put in the clock, and the button pushed to make a small mark on the clock's face. Every clock had to be back at The Woodman by six o'clock for the clocks to be "read" and the winner declared. If birds would not drop on the pen, upon their return, they were headed for the pot. If they landed on the house, Dad would throw bricks at them – sometimes missing and having to pay for new glass in the houses at the back of us.

There is nothing like letting the birds eat corn out off your hand, and watching them fly. When they turn into the sun it's like seeing diamonds in the sky.

Left: Sue Windmill's father, Don Morris (– seen working at Baggeridge Colliery in "Volume 1" page 179) - at home by the pigeon loft. Note the "pre-fab" in the background (no. 8A Ellowes Road), and the timing clock right foreground!
(Sue Windmill's Collection)

A Man and His Pigeons

By Julie Pitt

Pigeons, whippets, Woodbines and a flat cap are what I associate with my Dad. He was a typical Black Country man: his name was George Jones he was born in East Street Lower Gornal in 1922.His parents were Alf and Caroline Jones and he had brothers Alf and Joe, and Sisters Marie and Aggie. Apart from his family, his real passion in life was pigeon flying.

He kept pigeons for as long as I can remember and I was born in 1959. I remember when we were growing up, my Granddad used to come up our house to train the pigeons. When he was there we were not allowed to go down the garden or else he would go mad at us. He and my Mom had many a run in over this.

I also remember when my dad trained the pigeons. This included getting them to land in the pigeon loft as quickly as possible. He would release the pigeons let them fly around for a short while and then try to get them to land by shaking the tin with their feed in and shouting for them to come in. After a while they would usually have the procedure down to a 't' but sometimes they would land on the roofs of the neighbours' houses. My dad's way of dealing with this problem was to throw a small piece of dirt or brick at them. However, it was quite amusing when it landed on the next door neighbour's head.

My dad was a member of the pigeon racing club based The Old Mill in Upper Gornal. where the proprietor was a man named Norman Richards. When that closed he then joined the club based at The Fiddlers Arms. Every Friday night we would start the same ritual. Dad would choose the pigeons he fancied to do well in the race that weekend and put them into a large wicker basket. We would then take them to the pub to be registered. There the birds would have a rubber ring put on their leg and placed with all the others ready to be transported to where they would be released to fly back home the next day.

On the Saturday Dad would wait, armed with his tin of pigeon corn, and Mom acted as look out upstairs for the first pigeon to arrive. When they did arrive Dad would take the ring from the pigeon's leg, place it in a thimble and into a special clock where the time of the pigeon's arrival would be registered on a paper disc. Dad won lots of races including Federation ones where all the clubs in the area competed against each other.

I used to love to help him tend to the pigeons. This included putting flea powder on them, sometimes clipping their flight feathers or checking if they had been hurt during a race. This often happened if they flew into electricity cables. We would nurse them back to health by bathing and treating the wound for weeks on end. Dad knew all the tricks of the trade when it came to keeping pigeons including getting my Mom to bake grorty pudding for them or putting a platter egg underneath the hens to encourage them to lay their own.

Left to right: George Jones, Bill Jones, George's wife Gwen, outside the pigeon loft.
(Julie Pitt)

143

And about that pig…

In "Volume 1" it seemed a good idea to avoid yet another attempt to provide a definitive answer to that central Gornal question, "Who put the pig on the wall to watch the band go by?" However, while working on this volume a number of people have wanted to provide their own answer to the question. Could the answer come from the ranks of pig-keepers? I am indebted to Jim Fellows who provides the answer to the question by linking it to another local legend – the story of "The Gornal Thunderbolt."

Jim's father was James Fellows (1919 – 1990) who was a miner at Baggeridge Pit, and later a miner in the local clay pits at Milking Bank. He was married to Olive who worked at Clifford Williams, and they had two sons: Jim born in 1940, and Derek, born in 1947.

Just before one o'clock on Friday 24th October 1952 James and Olive Fellows were sitting quietly at their home – a stone cottage that was No. 4, The Alley. Suddenly without any warning there was a brilliant flash followed by a loud explosion. James Fellows was thrown across the room and broken masonry and shattered glass shot everywhere as the house was reduced to a shambles.

Neighbours rushed to help salvage belongings, believing that the explosion had been caused by nearby mining activity, but it was soon apparent that the house had been hit a by a freak thunderbolt. Neither Derek or young Jim were at home at the time.

Another casualty of this incident was Mrs. Hales' pig. The pig was terrified and tried to leap out of his sty – immediately opposite the Fellows' cottage. The pig ended up astride the wall with its leg muscles torn, and had to be destroyed – but not before its image had been noted by everyone present – this was definitely the pig on the wall.

The Fellows were given temporary accommodation by Sedgley UDC and after twelve weeks moved into a cottage in Ruiton Street. The Lower Gornal Athletic Football Club announced that the takings from the next day's game would be given to the family to help them get back on their feet. The thunderbolt soon became a local legend – and the death of Mrs. Hale's pig soon acquired the same status.

Below: When Jem and Hazel Fellows wanted a local product to sell in their gift shop in Abbey Road they decided to commission the manufacture of Gornal apple sauce boats in the shape of a pig. (NW)

Chapter 9
Scouts and Guides

In "Volume 1" we managed to include pictures of Scouts, Cubs, Guides, Brownies, Boys Brigade and Girls Brigade, but the emphasis was on 1st Lower Gornal Scouts and the 2nd Lower Gornal Guides and Brownies, but the definitive account of uniformed youth organisations in the Gornals still needs to be sorted out!

According to a February 1930 St. James' Church magazine there were Scouts and Guides at the church during that time, but the troops existing today are of more recent origin so there may be groups that have once existed in the Gornals but are already lost in the mist of time.

Right: The 3rd Gornal Brownies at The Straits. (Mary Jordan)

Below: The Zoar (2nd Lower Gornal) Guides on a trip to Wales. This is a troop that no longer exists.

The 2ⁿᵈ Lower Gornal Scouts

About 1976 Father Roderick Hingley, the Curate at St.James' Church, decided that it would be a good idea if someone could be persuaded to start a scout troop. He went to Julian Woodhall, of Temple Street, and suggested he was the man to undertake this. Julian accepted the challenge and became the troop's first Group Scout Leader, assisted by Ian Cox (Scout Leader), and Don Middleton and Martin Woodfield. Subsequently Judith Cox led the Cubs, with assistance from Jane Pickerill and Stephanie Darby, nee Pickerill.

The troop was started with seven boys and probably the leaders had little idea of the way in which scouting would take over their lives. Looking back, what is remarkable is that so many have ended up giving very long service to the movement – three have given over thirty years of volunteering! The troop has been going so long that it can take a long view of its history – with various ups and down, distinct phases, and an amazing continuity where subsequent generations have joined the troop, grown up within it and have returned to take part in its leadership or provide further generations of members. Until recently the troop was the largest in the district.

As well as "uniformed leaders", such groups also need volunteers as chairmen, secretaries and treasurers.

Julian's wife became group secretary and is still in that position today. Arthur Smith was the group's first Chairman, and his wife became treasurer. There have only been four chairmen and three treasurers in the group's life. Alison Lacon is the present treasurer. Other key names include Betty Smith, Geoff Taylor, Andy Spinks, Kevin Yates and Suzanne Jones. About twenty years ago the Scouts became "mixed" and sometimes girls have predominated in the troop. For the girls who prefer a single-sex group, Guiding has also existed at St. James'.

The group has engaged in every aspect of scouting; camps, gang-shows, bonfires, swimming lessons at Ellowes School, and taking part in the local carnivals and parades. The group was mobilised by the purchase of a second hand coach called Herbie and its successor, and these vehicles became well known in the Gornals. Later, when the group went abroad to camps they travelled in Walter Mills' coaches.

The troop has always met in the hut behind the "Mission Building" adjacent to the Memorial Hall and one of Julian Woodhall's early tasks was to make this building more usable. Up until the age of thirty six his life had been football but scouting well and truly took over and his "can-do" approach helped make the venture a success. Julian died in 2009, and the lower church gate is dedicated to his memory. His grandson has recently joined the Beavers.

Opposite page:
An early picture of the cubs and scouts of the 2nd lower Gornal Troop about 1978.
The back row includes the first leaders: Julian Woodall, Martin Woodfield, Peter Wood, Rev. R.S.P. Hingley who had asked Julian to set up the troop, Arthur Smith, Stephanie Pickerill, Don Middleton, and Ian Cox, in the Memorial Hall.

Above: Cubs pose for a picture in front of the Scout Hut built behind the Memorial Hall.

Back row: Maureen with flag, Jonathan Taylor as a Scout, Julian Woodall, Betty Taylor, Nick Smith, and Jane Green who is still a leader today.

(All pictures supplied by Mary Woodall.)

Right:
The Venture Scouts in the scout hut:
Leaders: Peter Woodall and his wife, Michelle (then Douthwaite), Middle row, left: Suzanne Jones who now runs the group.

Above:
The Cubs and Scout Hut. Leaders left to right: Val Jones, Jane Pickerill (Cub Leader), Julian Woodall, Betty Taylor (Chairperson) and ? About 1990.

Below: An awards evening in the Scout Hut: L-R: Frank Armson (District Chairman), Fred and Joan Cole District Scouts Commissioner and Cubs Commissioner , Julian Woddall, Andy Spinx – who replaced Betty Taylor as Group Chairperson, George Cox, and David Moss (District Scout Leader). 1999.

Above: Valerie Jones retires from scouting after more than thirty two years with the 2nd Lower Gornal Scout Group in 2014. She is seen with Nathan Sidaway and Suzanne Jones – her successor.

Valerie was drawn into scout-leading when her son Gavin joined the Scouts in 1963. (He, in turn, became a Leader.)
Below: The second "crew-bus" acquired by the 2nd Lower Gornal Scouts.

The 2*nd* Lower Gornal Scouts at an International Camp at Kandersteg in Switzerland in 2000. (All pictures supplied by Mary Woodall.)

The 1st Lower Gornal Guides first met in January 1975, in the Memorial Hall. It was started by Barbara Brotherton with help from Doreen Dunn, with Cynthia Jeavons running a Brownie Group that was already established.

Above: The 1st Lower Gornal Guides in 2005 with Annika Nahar (nee Patel) on the left and Chris Spencer on the right. Chris Spencer started to help when her daughter joined in 1985 and subsequently became Group Leader.

All pictures supplied by Chris Spencer)

Right: A Guiders' Garden Party organised to mark the retirement of three leaders: Wendy Jones, Janet Shuard and Eileen Beattie. Left tro right: Margaret Evans, Doreen Dunn, Helen Smith, Jenny Davis, Chris Spencer, Nicola Green, Chris Davis, Annika Patel and Sam Brown. Front row: Libby Presley, Wendy, Janet and Eileen, Liz Crawford, and Lesley Brookes, representing four out of the five groups in Gornal.

Contrasts in Guiding: Above: Guides in uniform from the 1ˢᵗ Lower Gornal Group play rounders on the ground behind the Memorial Hall in the 1980s. Below: The group today (2015) present themselves in less formal style.

Above: Guides celebrate Hallowe'en Night at the
Memorial Hall in the early 2000s.
Below: Combined Brownie Groups within the
"district" mount their Christmas Show at Himley
Road Methodist Church in 1995.

(Both pictures supplied by Chris Spencer)

Above: Janette Brettle retires from the 2nd Lower Gornal Brownies on 22nd January 1992, photographed in the small hall next door to St. Andrew's Church in The Straits.
Below: The Rainbows photographed in the Memorial Hall in 2005.

Chapter 10
Carnivals

Before the First World War most Black Country towns were home to carnivals and parades organised by local Friendly Societies. After the First World War carnivals were more often organised to raise funds for the local Hospital Committees but enthusiasm for them began to wane by the early 1930s. This seemed to be the case in the Gornals.

In 1952 the Gornal Carnival was revived – this time organised by the Lower Gornal Athletic Football Club, to raise money for their funds. At that time the club was £1200 in debt, and needed to clear that debt before spending money on improving the grounds at Garden Walk.

Albert Sargeant and John Timmins were Secretary and President of the Football Club and played the same role in organising the carnival. Esme Darrick was chosen as Carnival Queen by a committee of George Harrison (Chair of Sedgley UDC) and his wife, Rev. R.N. Timms (Vicar of St. James'), Mr. H.J. Jones (local bank manager), and Mr. B. Rowley, a local publican.

Below: Twenty-six year old Esme Darrick, of Summitt Place, was the Carnival Queen in 1952, seen here on the horse-drawn carriage with Aubrey Share in a jester costume. We can also glimpse the back of Councillor George Harrison, Chair of Sedgley UDC.
The carriage left Red Hall Road at 2.pm in glorious sunshine. (Rhona Pickerill Collection)

Esme Darrick was born in Birmingham but her mother came from Gornal. She had sought a career on the stage but had returned to Gornal and became a clerk in a local engineering firm. Her attendants were Iris Raybould and Jean Sadler.

The carnival was held on Tuesday 3rd June - the day after Whit Monday, but the fun had started on Saturday night with a dance at the Memorial Hall. Music for the procession was provided by the 3rd Worcester Battalion of the Army Cadets, and the St. Johns Ambulance Band, and special displays were put on at the stadium by the Red Hall Street Evening Institute's PE team, and the Sedgley Hand Bell Ringers. There were floats and fancy dress competitions galore and about eight thousand people went into the stadium where the event ended with a firework display. Albert Sargeant had hoped to make £200, but made more than twice that.

The success of the 1952 Carnival confirmed that community spirit was alive and well in post-war Gornal and ensured that the Football Club would continue to organise such events for the next two decades. Unfortunately it does not seem that anyone has kept a comprehensive record of them.

Gornal Carnival

Above Left: Carnival Queen of 1955: Wendy Smith. Above Right: Carnival Queen of 1956: Iris Powers.

Left: The 1956 Gornal Carnival: The Carnival Queen's attendants, Norma May and Miriam Shelton, seen in their carriage in Abbey Street. (Wilf Barrett)

Left: The carnival procession of 1956 turns into Abbey Road and passes in front of the Zoar Chapel, watched by the crowds. A Wolverhampton Corporation bus or two can be seen waiting at "The Duckle" on the right. This is the only photographic record the author has ever found of the Wolverhampton Corporation's vehicles in Lower Gornal! (Wilf Barrett)

Gornal Carnival

Above: John Timmins, President of the Football Club and the Carnival Committee, and Councillor Stan Dews, Chairman of Sedgley UDC stride out across the football ground in 1966. The pit banks and rising ground in the background are now covered in housing. (Wilf Barrett)

Above Right: A carnival float inspired by television's Black & White Minstrel Show. Mary Jordan, who supplied the photograph is sitting second from the right. (Mary Jordan)

Centre Right and Bottom Right: Kath Smallman, nee Turner, supplied these two photos of the "Harem Girls" taking part in one of the early post-war carnivals, and using Bert Hale's lorry to take part in the procession. May Witton led the girls, which included Edna Malpass and Sally Kenny as well as Kath herself. (Kath Smallman)

The 1958 Carnival

The 1958 Carnival may have been the best attended of all the post-war events – over 9000 people attended as measured by the number passing through the turnstiles at Garden Walk. Carol Garbett (from Macclesfied!), who was the 1957 Carnival Queen, crowned local girl, Dorothy Hale of Prospect Road, as the sixteen-year-old Carnival Queen. In honour of John Timmins' decade of work for the Football Club the ground at Garden Walk was named "The John Timmins Stadium" as part of the carnival proceedings. Among the many activities organised was a Skiffle Group competition – and this was won by The Black Diamonds, from Wolverhampton.

On the day after the carnival, whippet racing took place at Garden Walk.

Right: Fancy Dress competitions were always a popular feature of the carnival. Mohatma Ghandi thus appeared at the 1961 event!
(Joanne Robinson/Sue Windmill Collection)

Left: The Carnival Queen makes her way along Louise Street during an identified carnival. Note the scout leader with the collecting tin on the other side of the road.
(Mary Woodall Collection)

Bottom left: "Herbie" – the bus used by the 2nd Lower Gornal Scouts, based at St. James', passes Megan's shop in Louise Street. "Herbie" was an ex-railway crew bus bought at an auction. At the auction Betty Taylor shouted out, "We want it for our scouts", and it was promptly knocked down to her with no further bidding! Her husband, Geoff Taylor, subsequently had to maintain it, as well as being the troop's canoeing instructor!
(Mary Woodall Collection)

These two pictures of an early Gornal Carnival were taken as colour slides by Malcolm Palmer. Above we see a float passing Hemmings Bakery on the corner of Abbey St. and New Street.

These two pictures, which appear to be of the 1952 carnival, were taken by William Burrows as colour slides. Above: we see the parade making its way up Temple Street.

Below: A Bert Hale lorry transformed into a carnival float turns into Stickley Lane during the procession. (Pictures made available by Paul Burrows.)

Chapter 11
Gornal on Wheels

In "Volume 1" great use was made of photographs of the Wolverhampton trolleybuses passing through Upper Gornal on the No. 58 route, as such photographs often include such intriguing glimpses of their locations, and remind us of the variety of Gornal's transport scene.

Above: Wolverhampton Corporation Transport Sunbeam trolleybus no. 408 pauses at the Green Dragon on a tour on 5th April 1964, having just used the reversing loop in Jews Lane. The houses in the background, in Jews Lane, are still there today.

Right: Daimler Motor bus no. 514 stands in Wolverhampton waiting to take the no. 66 route to Gornal Wood via Penn, a route introduced in 1950.

Left: Midland Red bus no. 456 rests at Dudley Bus Garage after working the D6 service to Gornal Wood via Himley Road. The D6 route was quite "tame" compared to the D40 route which reached Gornal Wood via Eve Hill, Dibdale Lane, Lower Gornal etc. This route was quite notorious in the days when Bagley's Lane (beyond Dibdale Lane) was full of potholes, where it passed through Gibbons' works.

Centre Left: Deregulation of bus services and their operation has produced new colourful scenes for those who try to follow Gornal's bus services.
The Duckle – Gornal Wood's "bus station" - is home to three operators in this 1994 picture. A West Midlands Travel bus is in the background on the 137 service, obscured by the tail of a Metro-West Leyland National. (Jim Houghton)

Below: The experimental Guy "Wulfrunian" bus operated on trial by Wolverhampton Corporation Transport has just turned round at the top of "The Straits" about 1960, surrounded by hedge-rows where housing now exists. (Roger Taft)

Top left: Walter Mills coaching business was described in "Volume 1" pages 169-173. Their advertising often featured the latest additions to the fleet. This advert appeared in St. James' Church magazine.

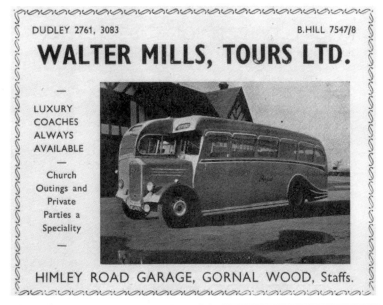

DUDLEY 2761, 3083   B.HILL 7547/8

WALTER MILLS, TOURS LTD.

—
LUXURY
COACHES
ALWAYS
AVAILABLE
—
Church
Outings and
Private
Parties a
Speciality
—

HIMLEY ROAD GARAGE, GORNAL WOOD, Staffs.

Centre right: Julian Woodall hired this Walter Mills Volvo coach on a "drive it yourself" basis to take the 2nd Lower Gornal scouts to an International camp in Switzerland. (The driving was shared with one of Mills' own drivers.)

Below: A Daimler half-cab coach, with Willowbrook body, of 1948 vintage. Was used on works services until 1960.

(Photos from the Walter Mills / Daphne Share Collection)

Commercial Vehicles

Above: A 1920s fleet of Baggeridge Coal delivery lorries.

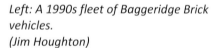

Left: A 1990s fleet of Baggeridge Brick vehicles.
(Jim Houghton)

Left: Slight camera shake has affected this photograph but it shows Hyde's Transport's early love of Leylands, and shows the fleet was always well turned-out.
(John Wilkes collection)

The Hyde Family are featured in the "People" chapter.

RF 6863, looking very smart in a David Hyde livery, poses in the quarry. (RF were the letters used for a Staffordshire registration.) (John Wilkes collection)
Below: Billy Waterfield, on the left, as driver of an early David Hyde charabanc parked outside the office in the Middle Quarry, off Pale Street, Upper Gornal. (Valerie Thomason)

Above: David Hyde's company lines up on the eve of nationalisation in 1949: Left to right: Bob Hodgetts, Billy Waterfield, Reg Cartwright, Ted Lees, Horace Thompson, Roland Hyde, Sam Hyde, Jimmy Hodgetts, Fred Hill, Billy Hill, Walter Hyde, George Walker, Fred Wilkes, Billy Porter, Tommy Sproson, John Wilkes (aged three), Abner Hyde and Walter Burgess (Abner's brother-in-law). The lorries are a Leland Comet, a Leyland Lynx and a Leyland Beaver. Photographed in the "Middle Quarry".

Below Left: Hydes Tours – examples of the early "charas". (John Wilkes) *Bottom right: Roland Hyde's AEC sixwheeler of later days.* (Sheila Hyde)

Chapter 12
Families and Individuals

Local Families

This chapter takes a look at one or two local families, and then individuals. Obviously one cannot take a look at them all, so these ones are simply "case studies", chosen to illustrate the way in which everyone and everything in The Gornals are inter-related, by family and marriage.

It is this "inter-relatedness" that helps Gornal preserve a sense of community that must once t have been a feature of all Black Country communities.

Below: The Bennetts

Henry Bennett and Matilda Woodhall were married in 1876 and had ten children. They pose here in 1918 at 47 Lake Street, Lower Gornal. It has been set in genealogical detail by John Carter and shows that, by marriage, the Bennetts were related to Tighes, Perrys, Wattons, Mills, Southalls and Marshes.

William Bennett became a fruiterer of Upper Gornal, Eliza Mills had a shop in High Holborn. Alice Bennett, not in the picture, married into the Hemmings – another local dynasty. Henry Bennett described himself as a "contractor's labourer".
(Vivian Smith)

The BENNETT FAMILY from Lake Street, Lower Gornal, in 1918

Above: This picture of Richard and Sussanah Bowyer outside No. 5 Straits Road arrived only just in time to be squeezed into "Volume 1" (Page 199) – but is used again here as it such a good family photograph.

Their son, John Bowyer, centre of back row, and his two sons were associated with the butchers shop in Abbey Street. Eventually a Richard Bowyer marries Megan Turner, in 1952, uniting two dynasties.

Left: The Hughes family of Tansey Green. Standing on the left is Ann Hughes , she and Bert Hughes went to live in Lower Gornal by the Five Ways. Their son, also Bert Hughes, ran a coal delivery business – see page 102. This ran form the other half of the house, more or less on the site now occupied by the British Legion Club. Louie Hughes (right) married Bill Moore, the Upper Gornal postman and became a midwife that everyone knew as Nurse Moore.
(Lily Porter)

The Wattons

In "Volume 1" a page was devoted to the salters and hawkers of Ruiton in recognition of their iconic place in the history of this small patch of Upper Gornal. Their nomadic way of life, moving off from Ruiton in the Spring to sell their salt, sand, and hardware, and returning in the Autumn, was fast disappearing by the outbreak of the Second World War. Particular families were associated with this trade, and the Wattons were perhaps the most widely known, but of course they married into other local families and the usual interlocking jig-saw picture of local life emerged. One or two people kept the way of life going into the post - Second World War era, but they are becoming difficult to trace when trying to establish links to this aspect of the past. In this respect it has been interesting to meet ninety year old Constance Revitt, nee Watton and learn that from the age of three she had travelled with her grandparents; William Watton (1868-1932) and his wife Constance (1880-1933). From this meeting a small part of the Watton family history unfolds.

Contemporary Watton family historians have traced their ancestry back to the seventeenth century so you can imagine what a large "family tree" can be drawn, but let's start with Con's grandparents. William Watton was born in 1868, son of anther William Watton (1812-1878) who had described himself as a "nail-hawker". His predecessors had described themselves as nailers, and it was in that time that some local families associated with the nail trade must have progressed into hawking.

Above: William Watton (1903 – 1964), of 13 Hill Street, Ruiton, with his cart, loaded with pots and pans, and his horse Shirley. He was the father of Constance Watton, who provided us with a starting point with which to look at the Watton Family

Below: The house in Hill Street. A shop next door was used as stable and store.

Con's grandfather was one of at least four children. His sister, Ann, for example, married a William Harper – giving us an example of how local families inter-linked. (See Trevor Genge's first Sedgley book, where the Harpers can be seen working in the quarry.)

William and Constance Watton had eight children, the first of which was also called William Watton (1903-1964) (aka as Billy Sheepo or Billy Conner). He married Louisa Groom from Coseley in 1924. He became a bricklayer, another trade much associated with the menfolk of Upper Gornal. William and Louisa had eight children, the first-born of which was Con, with whom our story begins. As we have seen, Con once travelled with her grandparents "with her combs and brushes over her arm", but Con's generation moved into a variety of occupations and moved to other parts of the world. Her sister Beryl, for example, became a teacher and became a headmistress. Interestingly, Beryl briefly worked at the Upper Gornal Board School, where she had once been a pupil before going to Dudley Girls High School, and found herself teaching her own younger sisters.

Above: Our enquiries centred on Con, third from left, sitting here with her youngest sister, Sue (second left) and daughters Janet (left) and Carol (right). Con, born in 1925, takes us back to travelling days, as she recall travelling with her grandparents.

Top left: William Watton, standing, aged fifteen with his cousin – Joe Jiggy Watton. William was often nick-named Billy Conner the" Conner" coming from his mother's name – Con.

Centre left: William with his horse and cart.

Bottom left: Louisa Watton with her daughter, Sue, on the right, and granddaughter Carol (Con's daughter) on the left.
(All photos from the family archive)

Right: Sue Watton married John Farron on 24th June 1967 and here we see the family at the reception, held at the Co-op Guild Hall in Upper Gornal.

Left to right in the front row: Ann Watton, Sue, the bride, Louisa – Pearl (Sue's sister), Louisa - mother of the bride, Constance, Mary Lilian and Beryl. (Beryl went to Dudley Girls High School, trained as a teacher, and found herself teaching her own sisters at the Upper Gornal Board School!)

Mary emigrated to Australia two years after this picture was taken. Increased social mobility and dispersal are all a feature of local families. At the back: Tim Watton and Joe Watton.

Centre right and below: Joe Watton, seen in the top picture,, married Monica Davenport at St. James' church on 17th October 1964. Joe (born 1943) and Tim, his best man (born 1932) were sons of William and Louisa Watton. The bridesmaids were Susan Parker, Janet Flavell (Seen on the previous page!) and Rita Flavell – both daughters of Con. (Note: the photo provides another glimpse of "The Limes" on the other side of Church Street!)

The Hyde Family

Let us begin with Job Hyde, of Upper Gornal, a carter of sand and local coal dealer, who died on 15th February 1888 at the age of sixty. He and his wife Sarah, had seven children: Jess, David, Job, Herbert, Bella, Clara and Quilly. At the time Job's death, his sons David and Jess were already following in the family tradition by being coal dealers. In fact they iherited their father's horses and carts to continue in the business.

David (1863 – 1927) and Jess operated as business partners for a while and owned nearly fifty horses. The business grew into general haulage contracting, but Jess left to become landlord of The Summer House, a pub at Swan Village. David Hyde seems to have taken a break for a year or two but then bought the rights to Waterfields' "Hartlands Quarry", also known as "Cricket Field". This became his new specialism and he later took over The "Middle Quarry" and one of the Holloway quarries, of Ruiton.

David Hyde married Mary Hampton in 1883 and built a house, plus stables and sheds, in Pale Street. The house included a verandah at the back where he established a bake house and Mary was able to sell bread from the premises. The Hydes prospered and stone from the quarries was used in the construction of many local buildings, after being dressed (or "scabeled") in the quarry. Sand was also supplied for furnace lining in local ironworks, and eventually for sale world-wide.

Eventually the Middle Quarry became "worked out" and the old mill house was used for garaging a lorry. This was about 1916 and this "Garner" lorry led David Hyde into his next veture. Ironically many of his horses had been requisitioned by the Government, and this venture into the use of a lorry precipitated David into the haulage business once again. By 1922 there were only two horses left.

When David Hyde died in 1927, the quarries at Hartlands and Holloway Street were still working but the haulage business had over twenty lorries and some charabancs. Meanwhile his brothers had moved on as well. Job, a bricklayer, had married a Harper, and Herbert was a carpenter in a self-built workshop in Club Row.

David and Mary Hyde had seven or more children: Lily, Abner, Mary, Sally, Sam, Katie and another Quilly. This is where the story begins to connect up with a story begun in "Volume 1" where we described Sam's and Abner's haulage business and how Roland carried on the tradition into the next generation.

Sam and Abner continued to run the haulage business built up by their father, and lived next door to each other in Rock Street. Sam married Ethel Bassett, and readers who like making connections will recognise her as mother of the lady who ran a ladies-wear shop in Louise Street, Gornal Wood. Their daughter Gladys married Walter Mills – of coaching fame!

Abner (1887 - 1968) married Sarah Watton and they had a son called Walter. Walter married Mary, and their son John provided many of the pictures used here. The David Hyde Transport business survived until nationalisation in 1949.

Left: The view from the back of David Hyde's house in Rock Street, looking across Cricket Field towards the houses in Pale Street in the 1930s. This was enlarged from a tiny print exposed on a Brownie camera and is of poor quality but it's an interesting image!

Right: David Hyde (31st July 1863 – 14th February 1927) and his wife Mary Hyde (nee Hampton) (4th November 1865 – March 1939), at the back of their home at 35 Pale Street, Upper Gornal. They married in Coseley in 1883.
Behind them is the veranda where Mary had her ovens for producing bread sold from the front of the house.

(All photographs relating to the Hydes from the collection of John Wilkes.)

Below: A line-up in the Middle Quarry in 1949.
Left to right: Walter Hyde, Abner Hyde, Roland Hyde, Sam Hyde and Walter Burgess – the husband of Lily Hyde, Abner's sister. In front of Walter is John Wilkes, son of Walter & Mary Hyde.
Behind them is a Leyland Comet in the David Hyde Transport red livery. The office can be seen on the left. Other pictures taken on this occasion can be found in the "Gornal on Wheels" chapter.

Left: A young Abner Hyde (1887 – 1968) and Emily Turner. (1888 – 1981)
They married in 1911 in Dudley. They had two children: Walter and Mary, and lived in Rock Street next door to Sam Hyde.

Left centre: The Turner sisters: Ginnie, Emily and Florrie, daughters of Enos Turner – a coal hewer of New Street, Gornal Wood.

Right centre: Abner and Emily celebrated their Golden Wedding in 1961 with a party at the Co-op Guild Hall in Upper Gornal.

Left: The houses built by David Hyde about 1925 for his sons, Sam and Abner, in Rock Street. Note the location – where Rock Street ends and Hermit Street begins.

The Turner Family

There are several local families who probably deserve a book in their own right, and if we select such a family to look at in this book, it has to be a fairly brief outline of the family's story, but an excellent example of the way in which a family history interweaves with the story of a small community can be demonstrated by looking at the Turners.

As always it's a question of where to begin. Let's start in Abbey Road, Gornal Wood, in the middle of the nineteenth century. Sargent Turner (1821 – 1874), son of John (1788 – 1850), both miners, lived at 13 Abbey Road. The property is marked on the 1848 Tithe Map and survey, and remained in family ownership until 1967.

By 1852, amidst the miners and nailers of Gornal Wood, Sargent Turner, and son Alexander, established the butcher shop and slaughterhouse. In the 1851 census Sargent is described as "miner, colliery owner, inn keeper and butcher"! Sargent married Mary Guest on 31st August 1845, and they had ten children, not all of whom survived. Sargent subsequently became the publican at The Bulls Head where son Edward was born, and the Pear Tree Inn of New Street. He died at the Pear Tree on 25th July 1874.

When Sargent's oldest son, Alexander (1847 – 1901), moved to Great Wheeler Street in Birmingham, Edward (Teddy, Sargent's youngest son), and his new wife, Sarah Rider Brookes of Coopers Bank, took back management of the Abbey Road shop in 1890's, starting with nothing but a pig bench. Teddy (1864 – 1950) went on to own property throughout Gornal. Edward and Sarah, whom he had married in 1892, had seven children. Their third child was Edward Sargent (1897 – 1965).

Right: Edward Tuner (1864 – 1950)

Edward Sargent (1897 – 1965) married Sarah Griffin, and they had three children: Edward, Alexander, and Kathleen. Kathleen, born 1926, is still with us, at the time of writing, to give us a first hand account of working at the "famous" Abbey Road premises, and to explain some of the Turner story.

Meanwhile the Turners have been marrying into other local families to create that "interrelatedness" that is such a feature of Gornal. For example, Mary Elizabeth Turner (1885 – 1937) - a daughter of John Turner and Elizabeth, married Abraham Cornmell in 1907. The Cornmells have a mention in "Volume 1" in realtion to the shop at Five Ways (page 41). Their daughter Olive Verena married John Newey – associated with the garage and car dealership on Himley Road. This is just one example. Another thread concerns Agnes (1893 - 1979), Beattie (1899 - 1918) and Mary Turner, the daughters of John. Agnes married James Johnson and their son Geoff ended up for time running the shop at Five Ways. Beattie married Joe Turner (a milkman from another family of Turners!) and their story involves butchers shops in Dudley and surrounding area.

Above: Edward Sargent Turner (1897 – 1965)
(The family seems to have favoured "Sargent" as the spelling of this name.)

This is the period that can be recalled by Kath Smallman (nee Turner), born in 1924. *"I was born at 27 Zoar Street, a reminder that my grandfather, Sargent, had bought houses for all his children, and I went to Red Hall School and on to Dudley Girls High School. I left school at sixteen to go straight into the shop with Dad and Uncle Albert. I did a great deal of the extensive book-keeping, but really enjoyed the interaction with our customers, many of whom were miners, and some were women from the brickyards in their shawls. I gave birth to my daughter Sally after a hard day's work at the shop. I remember Nurse Griffin getting me upstairs and fetching Doctor Cunningham at 10 pm. I was allowed three days off!"*

Note that Sargent's brother Albert has a mention. Albert became a well known local councillor in 1948, becoming Chairman of Sedgley UDC in 1965. (See "Volume 1", page 188.) Albert married Violet Southall in 1925 and they had two children: Megan and Jack, who both play a visible part in the life and times of the Gornals. Megan was born in 1926 and she married none other than Richard Bowyer – uniting two Gornal butchers' dynasties! Megan, who died in 2011, is remembered for the dress shop in Louise Street (see page 45). Her bother Jack (born 1930) who also died in 2011, was equally well known for his retail exploits in Louise Street. (See "Volume 1" pages 71-72.)

To return to the narrative concerning the Abbey Road business: following the First World War, Teddy's son 'Sarge' (Edward Sargent Alexander Turner) who had married Sally Wilkes Griffin, and with brother Albert (later Councillor Charles Albert Turner) took over running E. Turner and Sons. During the war, miners had higher meat rations and Sarge was on the Meat Allocation Board, with other local butchers. Len Parfitt was head slaughterman, often providing pig bladders which several children used as footballs. He also delivered meat orders using the van or bicycle, which continued after Sarge's children Edward (Ted), Alex and Kath worked in the shop. The family worked every day in the shop, making sausages and preparing the meat. Market days, in Hagley, Wolverhampton and Bridgnorth, were just as busy as that involved long trips to purchase stock.

Above: Turners at work! Left to right: Mr. Harris, Sargent Turner, Len Parfitt, (slaughterman), Ted Turner and Albert Turner. The lad is Stephen Turner. All at work in Abbey Road.

Graham Smallman married Kathleen Turner in 1947 at the Zoar. Behind Graham is Edward Turner, behind Kathleen is Sargent and Ted. Far right on front row is Sally Turner.

Above: Another good picture of the Abbey Road premises and shop. On the left: Edward Turner, then Len Parfitt. On the right: Sargent Turner.

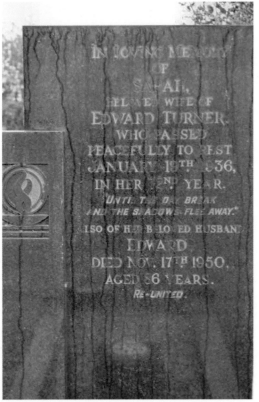

As the war came to an end, the shop in Abbey Street was being run by Sargent, his daughter Kath and son Alex (1932 – 1998). These were the last Turners to be associated with the business. The premises were sold to Ted Hodgetts – the son of Sargent's sister Frances. (Ted already had a butcher's shop at Rowley.)

The Turners' premises in Abbey Road were a key feature of the centre of Gornal Wood and many people have childhood recollections of going to see the animals awaiting their fate as an after-school pastime! Today the 1960s parade of shops and the corner premises of the Dudley Building Society do not seem likely to promote the same nostalgia.

Left: the headstone of the grave, in St James' churchyard, of Edward and Sarah Turner.
(The section on the Turners was compiled with the assistance of Sarah Turner from New South Wales!)

People of the Gornals

At the back of "Volume 1" is a chapter on some of the people of Gornal – not everyone, of course, but just a variety of people that others seem to remember. This section of "Volume 2" provides another selection - with apolgies to anyone who feels their favourite Gornal person has been left out! In order to avoid any issues about whether one person is more importan than another, they will be presented in randoml order of surname. The section will conclude with one or two Gornal people who played a part in local government.

Bert Box

Joseph Albert Bert Box is remembered because he built up a coaching business, starting in the spring of 1928, alongside his coal and haulage business, before Walter Mills dominated that scene. It seems likely that Bert began coaching by taking miners to the pit. At one time he had seven coaches, decreasing to five when he sold out to Hazeldine's of Bilston in 1957.

In the late summer of 1926 he married Monica Whorton, whose parents ran the Post Office at Five Ways, Lower Gornal. (The Whortons are mentioned in this respect in "Volume 1" page 45.)

Bert had two daughters, one of whom worked in the coach business's booking office which was in a sweet shop in Abbey Street. It seems that the sweet shop was run by his grandmother.

Above: Bert Box loved driving so it is appropriate to include a picture of him with his Austin car. It seems that he drove a coach whenever he could.
(Rita Walters)

Bert died on 10th June 1974, at the age of seventy four, and is buried at Gornal Crematorium. He was joined a year later by his widow Monica.

Left: Bert Box outside "Dabeth" – his home in Cinder Road, close to the yard where his coaches were kept. (Rita Walters)

Phone 3004 Dudley

Bert Box,

Haulage Contractor

Coal Merchant . .

Coach Proprietor .

PLEASURE PARTIES

Any Distance

Any Number.

A TRIAL SOLICITED

Abbey St., Lower Gornal

Above : Frances Fox and her Golden Voiced Girl of the Midlands trophy. (Mary Rousell/Rita Harrison)

Frances Fox

Frances Fox was born on 12th July 1912 and was born blind. She was the daughter, and sixth child, of William Henry Fox and his wife Hannah. Henry was a coal miner, and the family lived at 5 Garden Walk, Gornal Wood. Her mother died when she was only nineteen months old.

She undertook her education at the Royal Institution for the Blind at Edgbaston until she was nineteen and then went to the Wolverhampton & Dudley Institute for the Blind where she learnt the trade of machine knitting. From an early age she displayed musical talent and began piano lessons when she was five and later took up singing. She found she had a sweet soprano voice and started to take part in concerts. One such concert took place at Lake Street Methodist Chapel on 1st October 1933 when, at the age of twenty one, she sang at a prestigious organ concert featuring J.S.Moss. Two years later

later she won a competition to find "the Golden Voiced Girl of the Midlands".

For a time Frances lived with her oldest sister, Maud Stokes, but in the winter of 1946 she married Kenneth Stokes, who was partially sighted. A year after her marriage Frances applied for a guide dog and was eventually given Judy – a large golden Labrador. As a result of living and working with Judy, Frances became a speaker for the Guide Dogs for the Blind Association. She spoke at schools, churches, and many clubs, and became as well known in that capacity as she once was as a singer. Guide dogs retire at the age of twelve, and therefore Frances, who in later years lived at Central Drive, enjoyed the company of four dogs until the fourth retired in 1998. Frances died on 22nd. December 2000.

Alf Bradley

Alfred was born in 1900, the son of James and Mary Ann Bradley of Gatacre Street, Lower Gornal. His father was a bricklayer, and Alf followed in his father's footsteps. In fact he became a very good bricklayer and someone described him as "an artist in the laying of bricks."

Alf was known throughout The Gornals for his fine baritone singing voice. He joined the choir at St. James' Church when he was ten and remained in the choir all his life. At St. James' he was tutored by Howard Jones – choirmaster and organist and member of the "concert party" featured on the cover of this book. (See page 19.) Later in life he joined the Gornal Old People's Choir, formerly The Straits Silver Threads Choir.

For more than fifty years he was a member of The Cecil Lodge of the Royal Antediluvian Order of Buffalos in Gornal Wood, where he was also able to use his singing voice. (See page 132.)

He died in 1977 and is buried at St. James' Church. At the funeral 82-year-old Howard Jones, his old teacher and colleague, came out of retirement to play the organ.

William Burrows

For several generations the first born son in the Burrows family was called William, but the particular William Burrows who became the well-known printer of Lower Gornal was born in 1871, the son of William and Eliza Burrows. In 1891 we find him living with his widowed mother and step brother John at 30 Lake Street – and already a printer's compositor.

In 1899 he married Ellen Elizabeth Sutton, and two years later we find him living a 7 Summer Lane with a one year old daughter (Nellie) and describing himself as a "jobbing printer". This daughter died young but the Burrows went on to have a son named William John Sutton Burrows, born in 1912, and another son named Henry Archibald, born in the spring of 1914. The sons were expected to follow their father into the printing business.

It is not clear when William Burrows Snr. set up his own printing business, or when he moved this into the former chapel building at the corner of Lake Street and Humphrey Street. The chapel changed function when the new building on the other side of Lake street opened in February 1927. The old building did continue in use for few years as a Sunday School.

Nevertheless the Humphrey Street/Lake Street area became the centre of the family's life and William Burrows acquired other properties in that area. He also played an increasing part in the life of St. James' Church and became a Church Warden. He also appears in the photograph of the group of St. James' folk who put on plays and shows in the inter-war years. His sons also took up significant interests – William taking up photography and Archie formed a band! Meanwhile many of the jobs taken on at the

Above: Frances Fox in later life and her guide dog, Whiskey. (Mary Rousell/Rita Harrison)

Below: William Burrows (1871 – 1956)

printing works were done for local people, and organisations, eg. the parish magazine. We also know from the photograph reproduced here that William was at one time President of the Bilston District Provident Society – a "friendly society" set up in 1849 to provide illness and death benefits to its members, and later dealing in mortgages. The Society lasted until 1983 and seems to have been an important organisation of that kind.

William Burrows died in 1956, but the family are still represented in the Gornals by Paul Burrows, the grandson of William John Sutton Burrows. The printing business eventually left Humphrey Street to new premises in Tansey Green Road, Pensnett, and has since ceased to exist.

Left: Samples of William Burrow's photography: the family's cars in the printing works yard, and ox roasting at the British Legion.

Below: Archie Burrow's band at the Memorial Hall. (Paul Burrows Collection)

Doctor Cunningham

Donald Cunningham was born on 22 August 1901 and was educated at Bellahouston Accademy in Glasgow. His full name was Donald Elder Swan Cunningham, and he can found in the 1911 census living in Govan with his brother and two sisters. He graduated in medicine from Glasgow University in April 1924. For a time he travelled as a ship's doctor with the Blue Funnel Line – a Liverpool based company that conveyed cargo to and from the Far East. He then joined a general practice at Gartcosh before coming to Gornal in 1927. He returned to Scotland in 1928 to marry Barbara Hinds.

He seems to have first joined Dr. Fitzgerald and Dr. Mc.Millan, in Upper Gornal, and then opened a surgery in Summer Lane, in an building that later became Minnie Brecknell's hairdressing salon.

A 1932 directory lists him as having a surgery at The Limes in Church Street and at the premises in Abbey Road, while living at "Lyndhurst" in Humphrey Street. In 1936 he seems to be living, or practising, at The Limes in Church Street. A 1940 Directory lists the surgery in Abbey Road again, plus Westerlands on the Himley Road. The latter was his new home. His son Ian, born 1933, also qualified as a doctor and assisted his father with the work in the Gornals, and eventually lived opposite his father.

Meanwhile he helped many local people – leading to the fact that even today many people enjoy recalling their connection with him. For example, Kathleen Smallman (nee Turner) recalls: *"He was our favourite visitor. He came for a whisky at lunchtime, and was known to enjoy home-brewed ale. When Grandad fell down stairs at the age of ninety his prompt attention saved Grandad's life. Another time my brother Alex cut his leg with a chopper and Dr. Cunningham was on the scene immediately to stitch him up."*

Dr. Cunningham took to life in The Gornals and had a great interest in the language, customs, and local day-to-day life of the community. After listening to his patients, he became a proficient story-teller in his own right. He was also a bridge-player and enjoyed a round of golf.

The details of Dr. Cunningham's personal life after the Second World War are not so clear but it is known that he married for the second time in the summer of 1957. He married Doreen Alison Caddick in a local ceremony. What is clear is that Dr. Cunningham continued working for the people of Gornal – no one has ever said that he "retired".

Dr. Cunningham died on 1st July 1971, the day after his son Ian had left to work in Scotland. His funeral service was held at the Zoar Chapel and the place was packed – such was his popularity. A committee was set up to raise money to do something to reflect local feelings. This was led by Sheila Gamston , among others. They raised over £1000 and this was enough to create a memorial garden at the Health Centre and provide some improved facilities at the Darby & Joan Club in Abbey Street. On Sunday 26th November 1971 a ceremony was held at the Health Centre in Bull Street to commemorate his life and service.

The ceremony at the Health Centre began with Rev. Allen Fisher welcoming everyone and Dr. W.N.Miller made a tribute. A memorial plaque was unveiled by Alison Cunningham and Ian, the doctor's son expressed his appreciation. (The Council was represented by the Deputy Mayor, Councillor J. Jones.)

(Picture supplied by Fiona Cunningham)

Above: Plaques at the Gornal Wood Health Centre in memory of Doctor Cunningham.

Sammy Jeavons and Samuel Jeavons

In "Volume 1" the short section of Sammy Jeavons managed to get the facts all mixed up – confusing two local men with the same name. We return to the subject to clarify and treat them separately.
Below: Samuel Jeavons (1898 – 1986)

Samuel Jeavons (1898 – 1986)

Samuel was the eldest son of Benjamin and Sarah Jeavons and was born on 27 February 1898. His first job was working in the coal pits which lay between Himley Road and Wallows Wood, but he soon became a tram conductor. This was his occupation on 10 May 1916 when he enlisted for the army, at the age of 18. He was attached to the 2nd Battalion of the Durham Light Infantry. At the time he was living at 7 Holloway Street Square. This information comes from his enlistment form.

Following his enlistment Sam went into Army Reserve and was then mobilized for duty on 2 November 1916 at Lichfield. He was posted to France the following year, and from family sources it appears he went into Belgium where he was fortunate to have decided to spend the night in a field alongside the troop train which was blown up by the Germans causing many casualties. He is thought to have fought at the Somme. On 11 October 1917 he was transferred to the Labour Corps, the forerunner of the Pioneer Corps. They were manned mainly by ex-front line soldiers who had been wounded or taken ill or were enlisted men found unfit for front line service. We do not know how Sam qualified. On enlistment he was 9 stone 1 pound, in good physical condition, and classed B1 (able to undertake combat service). In the Labour Corps he was classed as B2 (only fit for lighter duties), but there is no explanation for this change in fitness. He was demobbed on 2 March 1919 and described as of 'good character`. His medal record shows that he received the Victory Medal and the British War Medal. The Victory medal was awarded to military and civilian personel who served in a theatre of war, and the British Medal for service abroad between 1914 and 1918.

After the War he continued to work on the trams and then the buses, ultimately as an inspector. Everyone using the Wolverhampton Corporation 58 bus, from Wolverhampton to Dudley via Sedgley, knew Sam Jeavons. He married Olive May Barratt around September 1927, and they lived in Kings Road, Sedgley, in her family home. She was born in Dudley in 1902. Subsequently they were divorced. There were no children. She may never have re-married because an Olive May Jeavons (born 23 September 1902) died in March 1991 in Kidderminster, aged 88.

For a while Sam went to live with his sister Betsy and her family at the Ridgeway in Sedgley. When he was 64 he married again to Elizabeth Eva Smallman (known as Eva) around June 1962. She was a widow and aged 58. She had lived with her sister in a top floor flat in Jockey Fields, Upper Gornal, and, after being married, Sam and Eva moved into a ground floor flat on the same estate. He continued to drive his car when he was over 80 and he died, aged 88, in May 1986. Eva then moved to the Hollies Residential Home (now Ridgeway Court) and finally to Rye Villa Nursing Home where she died in June 1993, aged 89.

Sammy Jeavons

Samuel Jeavons was born in 1902 and by the time we catch up with him in the 1911 census we find he is living at 25 Dudley Road, Sedgley, with his mother, Martha, a sister Beatrice and brothers Joseph and Charles. Martha had been a Watton and came from the travelling traditions of some Ruition folk. Sam's love of horses was probably inherited from both parents.

He appears to have worked in a colliery, and in particular worked with the pit ponies but his early working life is obscure. He is remembered as a "fruit and veg mon", based first of all in Pale Street and delivering from his cart to people in Upper Gornal and Dudley's Priory Estate. He made a special thing out of decorating his horse on May Day, and parading the horse as well as going on his round. He claimed to have started doing this when he was fifteen. Over the years this gained considerable media attention – hence the numerous photographs taken of Sammy Jeavons, his horses and brassware etc. Sammy had married Annie Elizabeth Jones, known as Lizzie, on 26th July 1926, having met her when she was on her way to work in a Pensnett brickyard.

Sam's family was reared at 35 Pale Street (Simeon, born in 1929, and Betty born in 1934), but in 1957, when the area was being "cleared", they moved to Pale Street, close to the Ruiton

Right: A portrait of Sammy Jeavons and his ponies by Graham Gough – a professional photographer who worked for numerous newspapers including the Express & Star, and the Dudley Herald – for over fifty years. The picture was featured in Graham's book, "The Black Country Album", published by The History Press in 2012.

windmill, from which he continued with his horse-drawn fruit and veg rounds. He eventually retired at the end of the summer of 1969.

Sammy was a keen member of the Royal Antedeluvian Order of Buffaloes and widened this interest to become a major charity fund-raiser. He developed a style of auctioneering for charity, and there was a great call for his skills at harvest festivals in many local pubs. He had originally been inspired by the Red Cross when he had taken his daughter Betty to appear at a gala held in Bantock Park, Wolverhampton. The reward for his charity work was a trip to Buckingham Palace on 2nd August 1976 to meet the Queen's Equerry.

Sammy is immortalised in a film clip broadcast by ATV Today on 1st May 1974, where he is interviewed by Gwyn Richards. We meet the family and the horse Trigger, who enjoys breakfast in the family's home. Sammy died in May 1986 and his funeral was held in St. Peter's Church, Upper Gornal. Needless to say, his coffin was carried to the church on a decorated horse-drawn cart.

Left: This picture of a very young Sammy Jeavons illustrates his life-long love of horses.

Below left: Sammy and his fruit and veg cart – the one he used in the summer – posed in Vale Street. Note the horse is decorated for Sammy's annual 1st May parade.

Below right: Sammy maintained a large collection of horse brasses and decorative harnesses – all of which could be put to good use on the annual parade.

(All pictures from Betty Caddick's Collection)

Above left: Sammy and his wife Lizzie.

Above right: Tony joins Sammy and his daughter Betty in the family home. This is immortalised in the ATV film sequence of 1974.

Right: Sammy's coffin driven to St. Peters Church Upper Gornal as part of Sammy's funeral. After the service a burial took place at Gornal Crematorium. The dray is driven by a Mr. Corbett, and is seen passing "The Arcade".

Bottom right: Sammy Jeavons was very keen on raising moneys for charity – particularly the Red Cross. He had this goat-drawn cart made for his daughter Betty – seen here at the age of about nine at a Red Cross event in Bantock Park, Wolverhampton during the Second World War. (The cart.was built by Tom Tighe.)

(All pictures from Betty Caddick's collection)

This famous picture of "Agenoria" – the locally built steam locomotive of 1829 vintage, which worked on the original part of the Earl of Dudley's Railway – is fascinating as a portrait of men as well as the machine. The bearded gentleman at the front of the tender is Joshua Mantle of a family much associated with the running of the line – but who are the others?

A Gornal family is convinced that the man with the white shirt-sleeves is their ancestor: Jeremiah O'Leary. His story provides a "case study" of an incomer settling in the Gornals and becoming part of the area's history.

Jeremiah O'Leary and his descendents.

Jeremiah was born about 1830 near Macroom, County Cork, in Ireland, the son of a farmer. He served in the British Army but when he later returned to the farm it was in other hands, and Ireland was facing the potato famine. He contemplated leaving Ireland for America but met two other ex-soldiers at the docks and they decided to leave for London. In London he became involved with work on the canals and this lead to him eventually finding himself at Shut End, near Pensnett. Possibly he worked on the Stourbridge Extension Canal which opened to Shut End in 1840. At Shut End Jeremiah met a widow named Ellen Hart whom he married on 1st January 1857, at the Catholic Chapel in Sedgley.

In the 1871 census we find Jeremiah and Ellen living at 39 Musk Lane, Gornal Wood. By then the family consists of Sarah and Edward Hart – the children from Sarah's first marriage, plus Mary, John, Ellen, and Jeremiah Jnr. – the children of Jeremiah. In the 1871 census, and subsequently in 1881, he is described as a labourer in an ironworks, but family tradition has it that he worked on the Earl of Dudley's Railway. He seems to appear in at least two photographs of the railway's famous locomotive, "Agenoria".

The name Jeremiah is then passed down the generations. Jeremiah and his wife Ellen had a son named Jeremiah about 1868. Their daughter Hannah , born 1872, later marries Joseph H. Oakley and they give the name 'Jeremiah' to their son in 1896. Jeremiah Oakley became associated with St. James Church and we see him in some of the surviving photographs of church activities, including the book's cover photo.

He becomes a member of the PCC for example. Jeremiah Oakley's sister – Hannah – married William Bradley in 1930 and their daughter Rhona, and grand-daughter Stephanie, live in Gornal Wood today: keen to explain the family history and show how the family's history is interlinked with that of St. James' Church, as well as the "original" Jeremiah and the Earl of Dudley's railway.

The sequence of Jeremiah O'Leary's life is still a little puzzling, and outside the family no one has been able to identify people in the Agenoria photograph, but the story still provides us with a picture of how people came to the Gornals and settled in the area.

Hiram Price (1915 – 2001)

Some people remember Hiram as the proprietor of a little sweet shop in Zoar Street, others remember him as a charismatic preacher.

Hiram Price was born in a little cottage in West Street when that area was still a hamlet mainly consisting of miners' cottages. He was the son of Hiram Price Senior and Louise Price, nee Flavell. At an early age he developed a love of reading and music. He wrote poetry which showed a spiritual side to his character and potential communication skills.

When he left school he worked for John Jones who ran a credit drapery side to his business in Zoar Street. Hiram was a credit drapery salesman and after acquiring a motor cycle he built up a round in the Shorpshire, and South Staffordshire villages. Later he went in the Army and after that he ran the sweet shop in Zoar Street.

In 1938 he married Florence Maud Bradley from the family associated with Lake Street chapel. Later Florence would look after the shop while Hiram was out on his travels. They had three children: Eva, John and Joy – all born at the family home at 51 Redhall Road. Hiram and Florrie were "inter-connected" with many aspects of Gornal life, and their children, and grandchildren all made their mark.

Eva Price, born 1943, went to Red Hall School, like her father, but went on to Brierley Hill Grammar School and Dudley Training College. She taught at Red Hall School and then went to Robert Street under Miss Southan - where she can be seen in the picture on page 78. In 1964 she married Reg Fellows and they eventually lived in a bungalow in Garden Walk that had been passed down from Grand-dad Bradley.

Eva, who assisted my enquiries while writing this book, died in September 2015.

Right: Hiram Price, whom Florence described as "The Dandy from Gornal"! He loved reading, music, and his Christian faith but also liked to look smart and was keen to try out the latest power-assisted cycles from David Whitehouse's shop.

Above: Hiram and Florence on their wedding day.

Amendments and Corrections to "Volume 1"

Please note the particular corrections:

Page 4: The procession is composed of people from The White Chimneys, not Gibbons workers as suggested.

Page 61: Top caption should mention Rhona Pickerill, not Rhona Pickles.

Page 66: The Darby and Joan club in Abbey Street did not open in 1948 as suggested. It was opened on 18th May 1957 – and I am indebted to Keith Harris and Gerald Pilkerton who alerted me to this and showed me an invitation to this event issued to Kathleen Gibbons. She is seen sitting to the left of John Timmins in the picture on page 66.

Page 83: The shop next door to Wise's was not Isaac Marsh's as suggested – it was a general store run by Luke Walters. In the photograph it is being used as a hairdresser, but went on to become Mary Bowater's chinaware shop and then a video shop. More about this shop when used by the Ball family is included in this volume.

P147: Top picture: The unidentified seated teachers are Albert Riley, Ann Mort and Avenell Flavell. The unidentified standing teachers are Margaret Kilby, Mick Dumbleton, Jim Astbury and Dave Jepson. Ann Mort supplied this information.

Page 151: Sorry – the picture is not of the Ellowes School at all! It is thought to be Alder Coppice.

Page 158: Margaret Sargeant points out that the only chap wearing a bow tie on the front row of the picture at the foot of page 158 is her late father—in-law: Jack Green.

Page 179: For lovers of detail: The pit pony shown on this page was named Joey!

Right murals put up to celebrate the Red Hall Schools' centenary. The school building contains several such artefacts.

The Red Hall Schools:

With these school located on two sites – on either side of Zoar Street – my comments on their history in "Volume 1" resulted in some confusion. David Eades, one time Headteacher at Red Hall Primary has pointed out several mistakes.

When the Red Hall schools first opened in 1880, in the present Infants buildings, there were three schools: Girls, Boys and Infants, each with a separate Head. As I stated, the boys moved across the road when the second building was completed in 1891.

In my list of head teachers on page 142 I omitted Mrs. Nicola Stanley who was head after Brian Dent for six years from 2007 until 2013 when Wendy Roche took over.

Page 143: Centre picture. Eddy Bake did not design the 1991 stone as I had suggested. Some centenary mugs produced by Ted Underhill used some artwork drawn by Eddy Baker in 1976.

Page 145: The picture used at the bottom of this page was taken in the Infants building.

Page 147: The lady standing next to David Eades in the photograph at the bottom of this page is Mrs. Jackie Blower – the School Secretary – not Miss Baugh as stated.

ACKNOWLEDGEMENTS

It seems entirely right and proper that the Acknowledgements should immediately follow a chapter on "People" because it is people who have made these books possible. I am very grateful for all the help, goodwill and generosity I have experienced while compiling the book. Some may have contributed just one photograph or one scrap of information, others have given considerably more help, but when putting together a jig-saw puzzle, all the pieces are equally important. I will try to list everybody I wish to thank but if anyone has been left out, I offer my apologies! I have listed people alphabetically by surname.

The following people helped me with the production of "Volume 1" but are listed again because so many of them have – by default – also helped make this volume possible:

Phil & Johnny Bagley, David Baker, Jean Baker, Norma Baker, Miriam & Ken Barber, David Bate, Philip Barnard, Jenny Beardsmore, Arthur & Jan Beddard, William Burgess, Alma Bowen, Ian Bott, Rita Brown, Michael Buxton, Bill Caldwell, George Blackham, Frank & Kathleen Bowyer, Muriel Brown, Irene Cartwright, Ken & Michelle Cartwright, Joan Cartwright, Mary Clark, Philip Corfield, Brian Cotterill, Margaret Cox, Roger Crombleholme, Bob Curtiss, Doreen Dunn, Angus Dunphy, David Eades, Lyndon & Margaret Evans, Colin Fellows, Mary Felton, Arthur & Jan Fithern, Cyril & Barbara Griffin, Gordon Grosvenor, Freda Guest, Jean Hinett, Steve Jackson, Pearl Juliard, Derek Jones, Les Jones, Martin Jones, David Haden, Derek Haden, Gwen Hadley, Arthur Hale, Colin Hale, John & Iris Hale, Anne Hartland, Janet Harvey, Rev. Fr. David Lloyd, Eddy Hickey, Linda Hickman, Stan Hill, Judy Hillocks, Keith Hodgkins, Mary Holmes, Ray Horton, Olwyn Hough, Jim Houghton, John Hughes, Jan Humphries, Elaine Hyde, Marion Hyde, Sheila Hyde, Bill Jewkes, Martin Jones, Ward Jones, Wendy Jones, Arthur Lee, Ron Leedham, Chris Lloyd, Johnny Longstomach, John Malpass, Gwen Marsh, Peter Massey, Keiron McMahon, Gladys and Raymond Morris, Dave & Sheila Moss, Joan Moss, John Moss, Dennis Neale, Don Newing, Eunice Parry, Malcolm Palmer, Marion Palmer, Brian Payton, Mike Perkins, John Prince, Margaret Sargeant, Gill Stewart, Harold Raybould, Paul Raybould, Eugenie Rhodes, Daphne and Bob Share, Verna Spittle, Di Swann, Bill Southall, Keith Taylor, Carol Thomas, Jean Thompson, Geoff Tristram, Clare Tolan, Jeremy Turner, John Wakelam, Rita Walters, Alan Wedge, Mark and Tracy Westwood, Norman Wheeler, Christine & John Wilkes, Janet Wilkinson, Bryn Williams, Vaughan Williams, Pat Wise, Margaret Woodall, Val Worwood. Liz Wright.

The following people have helped me complete this volume: Ruth Adams, Kath Baker ,Keith Bayliss, Ben Bennington, Liz Bentley, Helen Birch, Lynne Box, Paul Burrows, David and Margaret Boyd, Lynda Bridgwood, Betty Caddick, Graham Clarke, Stephanie Darby, Sue Farron, Vilma Eve Fellows, John Fellows, Graham Gough, Pauline Griffiths, Donald, Irene and Adrian Hale, Rita Harrison, George Harrison, Dorothy Hickman, Elaine Hickman, Roger Johnson, Diane & Terry Kinsella, Peter Lane, Monica Massey, Carol Marsh, Ann Mort, Jim and Pat Fellows, Alan Oakley, John Parker, Sylvia Payne, Rhona Pickerill, Julie Pitt, Joanne Robinson, Mary Rousell, Marion Savory, Kath Smallman, Gordon Smith, Vivian Smith, Roger Taft, Valerie Thomason, Gordon Tomlinson, Jim Watton, Joan Webb, Gary Westwood, John Wilkes, Joyce Wilkes, Melvin Wilkinson, Betty Williams, Sue Windmill, Mary Woodall.

I appreciate the information about The Gornals that has appeared in the Express & Star, one time Dudley Herald, and the Black Country Bugle. The staff at Dudley Archives & Local History Centre has been helpful in making material available. Roger Crombleholme has again produced the cover and Gill Morgan has looked after my well-being and joined me in exploring The Gornals. Bob Curtiss helps it all appear in print.

Local History in Print

Ned Williams has been writing and publishing Black Country history since the late 1960s and this is his fifty-first book. Many of the books have been published by The History Press, previously known as Sutton Publishing, but where the projects have been regarded as commercially unviable – like the Gornal books – Ned has had no alternative to publish the books in low numbers himself – using the name, "Uralia Press". Meanwhile he has regularly contributed to magazines like "The Blackcountryman" and for a time had a column in the Express & Star. He has also produced commissioned work like his "Part Three" of the history of the Walsall Co-operative Society.

Over the years his work has covered local railways, cinemas, theatres, fairground and circus, retailing (particularly "The Co-op"), chapels and town-based studies of Quarry Bank, Netherton, Brierley Hill, Dudley, Wolverhampton and now The Gornals. Ned's "day job" has been in Adult Education.

The Gornal books have sold via "Best Wishes" in Louise Street, Gornal Wood, and "Bywater's News Shop" in The Arcade, Upper Gornal. The Ashwood Garden Centre has also been a valued retailer.

Ned would like you to keep in touch and share interests via his website: www.nedwilliams.co.uk

Left: Over the years we have always tried to make book launches into something of an occasion. Here we see "The Gornals" being launched on 27th November 2014. Launches were held at the Zoar Chapel in the afternoon and at Upper Gornal Methodist Church in the evening. At the former we can see Bill Caldwell, Michael Hall (President of the Black Country Society), the author, and Ian Austin (MP for Dudley North), clutching their copies of the new book.
Books are available at launches, from local shops, and directly from the author.

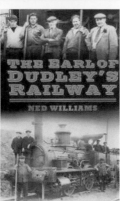
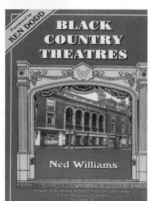